# REDEEM YOURSELF

## By Jerome Livingston Jr.

REDEEM YOURSELF
Copyright © 2012
Jerome Livingston Jr.

All Rights Reserved

ISBN: 978-0-9849455-0-4
Library of Congress Control No. 2012906328
PUBLISHED by: PJ COMMUNICATION

PRINTED in the U.S.A. by Create Space
7290 B Investment Drive
North Charleston, SC. 29418

To Thy Own Self Be True

Through the eyes of one who's been
redeemed, we should remain strong and think
positive. You ought to have faith and a strong
belief that everything will be alright. Turning
one's life around can be difficult but not
impossible. You need to have a strong
constitution to change.

# Contents

## Acknowledgement

I give God the glory for the great things he has done. Throughout the years, God has been good.

To my lovely (Wife) Mrs. Patricia Peeples – Livingston, after all these years, you remain my "beau" and the joy of my life. Thanks for believing in me and standing by my side. Troy and Shawn Livingston (SONS) and grandchildren, I wish you all good health and prosperity. To friends and family, you helped me make this book possible.

Vincent Hodge (COUSIN) I admired your strength and words of encouragement. Gilbert Livingston (BROTHER) I often think about you, you will always be remembered. Reverend Marshall Maxwell thanks for being patient and an understanding. You rest in peace.

Carol S. we have shared many good times and have overcome obstacles in life. Thank you for your friendship. Angelia Wilcox thanks for showing us around Savannah, GA. You help made our transition easy. Upon returning to New York, we manage to stay in contact.

Dr. Mae B. Sanchez it's a blessing knowing you, you sharing your knowledge and inspiration. Anchor House thanks for opening your doors and allowing me refuge. I am indeed grateful and owe you a debt of gratitude.

Jan Malloch: author, "The Positive Achiever" is a spiritual and inspiring book. Cassandra Mack: author and entrepreneur, I recommend her book "The Black MAN'S Little Book of Encouragement." It's an excellent reading.

Marc Williams, Assistant Principal, it is fate that allowed us to meet. Discovering that your degree is in English while seeking someone to read my manuscript, led me to believe that you, indeed, were that person. Thanks for your services.

# Introduction

Through the eyes of one who's been redeemed, we should remain strong and think positive. You ought to have faith and a strong belief that everything will be alright. Turning one's life around can be difficult but not impossible. You need to have a strong constitution to change.

The Civil Rights Movement began in the South many years ago. Civil right leaders fought for the rights of people. Leaders marched for equal rights, jobs, education, fair housing and the right to vote. Since Dr. Martin Luther King's death, we have lost much in his accomplishments and it appears his cause might've been neglected.

President Barack Obama has inherited the fall of America. The education institutions are falling apart, politics and the economy are in a shamble. This man became President at a time like this because much of the nation has failed its people, and he's expected to deliver America from its disaster.

The real crime in America are being committed by greedy people who manipulate government legislation, law enforcement practices and criminal justice policy to make youth commodities for other people to make a living and prosper. Economy! What we are witnessing and experiencing with respect to the economic situation in America is serious. We should not take for granted that everything will turn out alright.

Many citizens in the United States have lost confidence in the laws that are written in the United States Constitution. People are seeking solutions to some of the hardships they face today, while also attempting to learn about and regaining their Constitutional rights.

African Americans are involved in crime, substance abuse, suicides, incarceration, feelings of hopelessness and worthlessness, poverty, poor health and unrealized potential in academic and occupational pursuits. Until we address these crises in the Black community, youth will continue to die and not live up to their dreams.

How the laws are design to in trap young people, and how mass incarceration has become a billion dollar industry. I motivate people against incarceration and a guide to succeed upon being release.

We must provide an education that proposes our youth to become a viable part of society. They must have economic alternatives and practical reasons not to engage in negative, destructive behaviors. We have not helped young men to obtain the necessary skills to be successful in life.

One in three U.S. high school students drop out before graduating and more than 1.2 million students drop out every year. Statistics reveal students dropping out of school will cost the nation nearly three hundred thirty billion dollars over their life time in lost wages, taxes and productivity.

Pastor Sherrod speaks about slavery returning to America. Slavery has been abolished for over two hundred years. President Abraham Lincoln signed the Emancipation Proclamation for Negro people to be free. Slavery in America today is not working in the fields, picking tobacco or cotton. Prisons have become America's new plantation, where prisoners are force to provide cheap labor; they can be used to increase the economy.

Despite our enslavement more than four hundred years ago, our ancestors never gave up. They did have faith that the cream would once again rise to the top, but lately a sense of hopelessness seems to have invaded our spirits. This book will allow Americans to visualize their struggles to obtain the American dream, but denied various opportunities.

# HOW IT BEGAN

As I look into the mirror, it allows me to look deep within myself. I stood before the mirror, believing that I was having a spiritual awaking, but I cannot explain this experience. Drugs have caused me to become a slave, and experience the degradation of hell. Feeding an addiction, I did what was necessary to support a habit. There were multiple reasons or rationales to use drugs, but very few reasons or rationales not to use.

Making a change in life will not be easy. For years I been self destructive, and determined to do things my way, it seemed impossible to change. I feel that life has done me wrong. Certainly I was not born a drug addict or an alcoholic, and therefore determine to get sober.

I had previously resided at Anchor House. Unfortunately I did not complete the program, because I had a desire for the streets and had no intention of changing.

1

# REDEEM YOURSELF

For me hustling and using drugs was the norm. While leaving the program a counselor approaches me, if you have any problems you're welcome to return.

On October 1, 1981, I moved into Anchor House residence. Homeless, hopeless and had pushed myself to the brink of an emotional and physical death. I was afraid to be honest with myself about the fact that I needed to change. Eventually, my mind was made up; I was going to change and bring order to my life.

Those who come to Anchor House for treatment, do so in various ways. The court will refer people, concerned family members, friends, or institutions. Many are homeless individuals who simply walk in off the streets.

While all are seeking help for their addiction(s), often people need assistance for problems that go far beyond drug abuse. For instance, some people have been rejected by family and friends and feel abandoned by society. Other fined themselves with no more than an elementary school education or no marketable skills and realizes that they can't compete.

In the past only men with various problems were accepted into the program. Today, Anchor House accepts men and women into the program. It's an eighteen month program, for people with a drug problem, and for people who want to straighten out their life.

# HOW IT BEGAN

I can do all things through Christ which
strengtheneth me.
### Philippians 4:13

God looks beyond all of my faults. He and only he
can judge me. I am not perfect but I am progressing.
No one is without a blemish and it is not something to
be ashamed of. It's a reminder of a wounded past that
can be used to heal others. We all have defects and
weaknesses; after all, we are God's work in progress.

We may have been damaged, but that should not
give us a reason to be discouraged. There is always a
choice in times of afflictions. We can either choose to
be buried in depression or we can use the situation to
become a better person and be a good example.

Today! Know that no matter what has happened to
you and how badly you feel about it, as long as you've
got breath in your body you have the ability to turn your
life around. So today, wipe the slate clean. Put the past
in its proper perspective. Then, face life head on as the
undefeated champion you were born and created to be.

The program has a daily routine and daily devotion
sometimes twice a day. We are required to attend
church services. The daily required choirs include
making up your bed and cleaning the facility. Once a
month we perform detail cleaning, stripping and waxing
the floors. In the beginning I despised doing choirs,
because it was volunteer work and I did not get paid.

# REDEEM YOURSELF

But in time I learned to accept responsibility. These different duties would prepare me for a job.

I was sitting in the window staring into the night, it was Halloween and the children were out "trick or treating". One year prior on Halloween night, my aunt was murdered.

Aunt Geraldine was like a second mother, she meant the world to me. She was a great inspiration and always encouraged me, to straighten out my life. My aunt's death hurt deep down inside, she no longer can give me good advice.

A month in the program and I'm given outside privileges. It has been awhile since I seen the children, so I decided to pay them a visit, but uncertain if they were home. Troy came walking out the building as I approached; he's on his way to the store. We embraced each other with a big hug. Seeing Troy brought tears of joy; it's been awhile since we seen one another.

Troy! "Tell your mother we need to talk." He returned a short time later, telling me Yvonne does not want to talk. Nothing has change between us over the years. She continues to hold a grudge and is unable to forgive me. Dad! "Will you visit us more often, because so much is going on, and I need to see you?" "Yes! You will see me more often."

4

# HOW IT BEGAN

On Saturdays, Troy would visit me, but against his mother's orders. He enjoyed playing basketball, ping-pong and shooting pool. We got to spend quality time together. Yvonne had a great deal of influence over my son Shawn; she would not allow him to visit, due to her selfish reasons. The situation has made me angry but I will not give up.

During the weekend the men would stay up late, watching television and reminiscing about the good old days. But bad memories seem to out weight any good times. Many times I thought about leaving Anchor House. My thoughts made me think, I would not survive those cold streets. The streets do not provide you any love, dignity or respect.

As time went on, I began feeling good about myself, and had a desire to succeed. I look forward to attending Alcohol Anonymous, with a desire to get sober, but realizing this would be my greatest challenge. So, I began to identify with the speakers and learning to live life on life's term. I apply the twelve steps and twelve traditions in my life.

Second time in Alcoholic Anonymous I was sober one year. During that time a strong desire to smoke weed. You were not allowed, to talk about drugs in alcoholic Anonymous. Any discussions about drugs were not permitted. Narcotic Anonymous did not exist in New York in 1980, but did exist on the West Coast.

# REDEEM YOURSELF

It was springtime: the flowers were blossoming and the birds were singing. I never before recognize the beauty of nature. So many years I'd taken life for granted and did not appreciate God's creation. It is great to be alive and to appreciate the beauty in life.

Several months in the program and I suddenly get an urge for the streets. So, I had a plan to make some money, and decided to play a number, in hope of getting on my feet. I put seven dollars straight on five hundred. Upon entering the number spot I noticed 50 was out, so I anxiously awaited and hoping for another o, but instead a 1 played. The number not coming out made me very angry. But not hitting the number might've saved my life.

I knew Otis from the streets, on occasions, we had gotten high, and I seen what drugs had done to him. He eventually went to prison, and we had lost contact, but I often wondered what happened to him. I had not seen him in years upon entering Anchor House.

To my surprise, Otis is a counselor and he's sitting behind a desk. At first I thought it was a hustle, but later I realized God had changed him, I would've never expected him to change. He made a one hundred and eighty degree turn and his transformation is a miracle.

Otis decided to talk with me. "Jay! You are not ready to leave the program. Do not leave you are not ready. Listen to your heart; it will tell you when you're ready."

# HOW IT BEGAN

I immediately realize I'm not ready to handle any responsibility.

While lying awake in bed, I began thinking about my situation. I needed to rise above the drugs and the streets. The life I'd been living was no longer glamorous or exciting. It was time to become a better human being and do something positive in life.

Making a change is not easy. At that moment, I knelt on my knees and began praying, and asking God to give me strength. For many years my demons have haunted me. That night I slept peaceful and awaken with a sigh of relief. That morning I felt an inner peace and a desire to change.

If you are to win the game of life, then you must develop the attitude that nothing will stand in your way. This means that when one door closes, you must find another. If you cannot find another, go through the basement or work your way up the ladder. If you cannot go through the basement, revise your strategy and try again. Then, wait until an opportunity present itself. If an opportunity does not present itself, put your hustler's hat on and create your own.

I was attending Alcoholics Anonymous and talking about problems. People should change their old ideas, in order to acquire sobriety. It is suggested that you get a sponsor that's making meetings and working the steps.

# REDEEM YOURSELF

Mike became my first sponsor; he appears to have good quality in sobriety, and he's making meetings. Mike was constantly talking about the twelve steps and the twelve traditions.

I enjoyed going to 2230 fellowship. A place to socialize, and conducts daily A.A. meetings. After the meeting we'd shoot pool, play cards and dance. This is a wonderful place to get sober; I learned to enjoy life without drugs or alcohol. People came to socialize and to have a good time.

It had been nearly a decade since I had worked, but I managed to keep an income; however its time I sought employment, time to get a job and earn a living. Having a job will make you independent and afford you the nicer things in life.

Finding a job is easier than I thought. I meet a Jewish man at his place of business; he apparently seen something within me. Van gave me his phone number and said to give him a call. Upon returning to Anchor house I immediately called him. Van asks if I had a problem. I had no idea what he's referring to, so the thought of lying entered my mind; but instead I tells him the truth.

Sir! "I am a recovering alcoholic and a drug addict." "Do you attend meetings?" "I attend meetings regularly and have a sponsor." He surprises me, saying he's a recovering alcoholic. We have something in common. This addiction does not discriminate.

8

# HOW IT BEGAN

Van hired me for the job, so I need to show up on time, and be ready to work. This means going to bed early, to get adequate sleep and wake up on time. The boss will expect me to be on time. All my life rules and regulations never seem to matter. Showing up to work on time will show that I'm dependable and responsible.

The program teaches that half measure avails you nothing. You need to change your old ideas, of people, places and things. My life has taken a one hundred and eighty degree turn; no longer do I consider life a gamble; no longer do I blame everyone. For I realize that society owes me nothing. People often have a problem with change, because they have closed minds and find it difficult to accept change.

Theoretically speaking I burnt bridges, because I did people wrong, and as a result, I could not be trusted. People had given up on me; because I'd promise time and time again, to do the right thing. It will take time for people to gain trust in me.

People had given up on me, saying you're a hopeless cause who can't be helped. No longer could I be trusted and my word did not seem to matter. It reminds me of the story, of the boy who cried wolf. One day he told the truth about seeing a wolf, but no one in town believed him. People get tired of hearing you constantly lying.

# REDEEM YOURSELF

In order to gain sobriety I need to be sincere. There were moments I felt alone and had a desire to pick up, but decided not to give up. Feelings are not facts, so I'm learning not to respond to my emotion. Adhering to the suggestion in A.A. and applying the twelve steps in my life. It is a fact that I'm powerless over drugs and that my life became unmanageable.

With my sponsor I shared my darkest secrets. Charles would give me sound advice and direct me to the twelve steps. Speaking about certain matters in A.A. meetings, made me realize that I was not alone, and that people had similar situations.

People will think whatever about you regardless, whether it's good or bad. Family may turn their back on you. It would be a lie, to say it did not matter; we want people to like us. I have faced many situations in life, so I choose not to accept people(s) attitudes, or allow people to decide my fate.

Today, I know that no matter what happened to you and how badly you feel about it, as long as you've got breath in your body you have the ability to turn your life around. So today, wipe the slate clean. Put the past in its proper perspective. Then, face life head on as the undefeated champion you were born and created to be.

Stand up for what you believe in. If you really want to succeed, adhere to the rules and values that are important to you.

# HOW IT BEGAN

Do not let others persuade you to accept anything less than your own high standards. Aim high as far as your standards and principles are concerned.

Believe in your own high standards and you will achieve much in your life. Above all, you will be able to achieve happiness, which is the ultimate achievement, and you will be able to experience the wonderful joy of helping others along the way.

A man's responsibility is to self, his family and another human being. Spend time with your children; go to the park, go fishing and do other exciting things. My parents did these things with their children. Dad sometimes took us to Coney Island fishing; we spend countless hours fishing on the pier.

The job is keeping me busy; I'm cleaning offices and apartments. Having a job is a good feeling; I'm not earning big bucks, but I'm grateful to be employed. People should learn to crawl before they walk. I started at the bottom because I had no skills. Working will allow you a regular paycheck. The job is legal; there's no need to worry about the police arresting you.

First you need a desire to achieve, which must remain strong throughout. Be determined, and persistent. The second is ensuring that you express gratitude. Everything comes into your life for a particular reason. Take nothing for granted. Everything in your life has been given especially to you to help you learn, to progress, and to succeed.

11

# REDEEM YOURSELF

People making money should know how to adapt to situations. You make money, but do not allow money to make you. Fast money will bring on consequences, like being on the run and having to look over your shoulder. The Bible states, "For the (love of money) is a sin." And that means you will do whatever it takes to make money.

Develop an attitude of gratitude. Start paying attention to areas where your life is already prosperous. Be thankful for what you have while creating avenues for more. Notice the many ways that you are blessed. When you develop an attitude of gratitude an internal shift in your consciousness occurs allowing you to open yourself to greater blessings.

Yvonne continued given me a difficult time, she would not allow me to see the children. For years she has held a grudge against me and has expressed hostility towards me. A woman's scorn is wicked. She is not concerned about me being a father. As parents we could not come to terms raising the children.

In regards to Yvonne allow me to comment. She was a fun loving person, who did not expect much in life, she desired to raise a family. The life style I chose made it impossible, and difficult to settle down. We experience parenthood at a very young age.

My son's mean the world to me, so her lack of disrespect hurts, but I believe time will heal all wounds.

# HOW IT BEGAN

She has been hurt physically, emotionally and spiritually. I am willing to make amends, because that is the right thing to do. It takes a man to admit when he is wrong and to accept responsibility.

Every experience, every relationship, every aspect of your adult life is directly related to a choice you made or failed to make at some point in time. Very rarely do things just happen to you without there first being a choice that you made or failed to make.

The law of cause and effect teaches us that every choice we make today has ramifications on our tomorrow, next week, and next year and sometimes the rest of our lives. There is no way around this because everything you do in one area of your life ultimately impacts another.

Many people have conditioned themselves to blame something outside of themselves for the aspect of their lives that they regret or that they are unhappy with. They blame "the man," a difficult childhood, the job, the ex – wife, the baby's mama, lack of education or anything else that they can use as an excuse to not hold themselves accountable for their choices in life. Once you realize the power behind every single choice, you begin to think more long term about your decisions.

I'm willing to go to any length to seek sobriety, so therefore I had to change my attitude and not hold onto resentments.

# REDEEM YOURSELF

Should not be around certain people, places and things, such as bars, clubs, social gatherings, where people are getting high. I had to be aware of my thinking, because my mind would paint pictures of having good times. Listening to music or television commercials showing people having a good time drinking would sometimes bring back memories.

People would say you can get high, and assure me that everything will be alright. Jay! "You're the life of the party and fun to be around. Those people in A.A. don't know you; so what are they talking about? You do not have a problem. So right now you're just down on your luck, but you'll get it together. Jay! Come on let's get high."

The devil is constantly busy and refuses to release his prey. For years I've been the devil's soldier, doing his evil deeds. In situations today, I'll say devil, "get thy behind me." I am learning to lean on a higher power, that is greater than myself and that higher power is God.

Having a desire to change would become a challenge. Changing my negative behavior, I had to stop blaming people for my situation, or believing that society owed me something. I had to change my perception on life.

No matter what you do in life, you are always faced with a choice.

# HOW IT BEGAN

Everything you do in a day, and all of the results of your actions during that day, all depend on choices that you make.

It was nearly time to leave Anchor House, so I began looking for a crib with hopes of finding something nice. Soon I will be paying rent and dealing with responsibilities. Paying the rent will not be easy; due to an unmanageable life style, but I needed a place to live. So therefore with that in mind, I'll learn to pay rent. After work I went looking at apartments, I saw several apartments but none satisfied me.

A week later, I found a one bedroom apartment, in a nice neighborhood and the rent was affordable. The landlord requested one month rent and one month security in advance. Paying six hundred dollars presented a slight problem, because I had six hundred fifty dollars in the bank and that would leave me little money.

So doubts began to enter my mind, on whether or not I'd fall flat on my face. Trying will beat a failure any day. Rather than shying away from something complicated or difficult, keep the end result in mind and push yourself to get out of your comfort zone.

I decided to step out on faith, because only if you believe, all things are possible. I'd gone to the bank and withdrew six hundred dollars.

# REDEEM YOURSELF

The landlord accepted the money; he gave me the lease and keys. While standing in the apartment, I'm thinking about buying furniture. Various ideas came to mind on decorating the crib.

Graduating the program is indeed an accomplish - ment. Anchor House accepting me into the program is indeed a blessing and I am truly grateful. A few guys want me to give a speech. My road back was not easy – not by a long shot – but I receive the help at Anchor House. During the speech I got emotional, tears begin to roll down my face, but they were tears of joy.

The Director presented me with a certificate and a new set of dishes. Receiving the certificate was indeed special. For once in my life I completed something and received an award. A few counselors said a few words and wish me good luck.

We gathered around the table to say grace. The food is certainly delicious, and for desert, we had chocolate cake and ice cream. This would be my last dinner as a resident. Jay! "You are welcome to stop by anytime, and have a meal." So occasionally, I took him up on his offer.

While lying awake in bed, I begin to realize a transformation has been made. I have been trans - formed into a positive person. My attitude, thinking and behavior have changed. No longer need I live a lie, or have to keep up with the Jones, and live up to someone's expectation.

# HOW IT BEGAN

Learning to be a man and do what is required. I'm becoming responsible, trustworthy and dependable. I was going to work on time and doing the job. First rule in life is self preservation, which means taken care of yourself and your family.

Contrary to what many people believe, character counts. Character can take you where money, charisma and notoriety cannot. Today, make the decision to be a man or woman of character. Honor your commitments. Do what you say you're going to do and do it on time.

Don't always look for the easiest way out. Sometimes what is easy in the beginning comes with more problems than you bargained for later on down the road. Most of all, try to do the right thing, in the right way, so that your character speaks to others.

You don't ponder change, nor do you think about it and do not run from it. You must embrace transformation, because you have nothing to lose and everything to gain. A conscious effort to change will make you a better person. You gain a high self esteem of one self. You become a better human being and have a desire to do right.

Take control of your life and start enjoying the challenges that life throws at you! When you get up in the morning, decide that you will have a positive day.

# REDEEM YOURSELF

Count your blessings that you are here to enjoy another day. Imagine all of the wonderful, amazing things that will happen to you today. And go out and enjoy it!

Saturday morning and I'll be moving to a new apartment. It's a beautiful spring morning. I said good bye to everyone and called a taxi. The adrenaline is pumping and I am very excited. It's a joy knowing that I have turned my life around, and that I'm looking forward to the challenges of life.

I had no money to buy furniture or groceries, but I will survive these conditions. During this time I ate peanut butter and egg sandwiches, also I slept on the floor. I intend to rise above these conditions, so I would continue to believe and keep the faith, also remain strong in order to survive.

There is something about an individual who is willing to walk through fire and keep on keeping on, even though the cards are stack against him that makes others take notice and want to help.

The problem is most people give up when they encounter hard times, especially in situations that knock them off their feet. They look at their situation and look at all the obstacles. Then, they decide that there is no way they can make it. Then, they hang up their hats and give up on life.

# HOW IT BEGAN

A part time job is not enough for me, so I sought another job that would pay more money. An employer interviewed me for a maintenance position, and has decided to hire me. This position is also part time, but I accepted the position, its work that I'm interested in doing; also I had no real qualifications.

Working two jobs is not easy, a job on the east side and a second job on the west side. Every day I'm dealing with mass transit going to work. This task is not easy, but I do believe things will get better, and I am doing what is necessary.

If all you known are struggle, then you already have what it takes to make it. You're resourceful. You've got staying power. You've got a thick skin. You're resilient. What's more, no matter how hard life knocks you down, you always find a way to get back up.

Sounds like the makings of a winner to me. So, why not use those same skills that enabled you to survive in the concrete jungle, to help you rise and thrive in the corporate one? Use that same hustler's spirit to elevate your game legitimately.

Putting a few paychecks together I'm able to purchase a bedroom set and a dining room table. While shopping I happen to notice a living room set, but I'll purchase it another time. Sir! "Your furniture will be delivered on Saturday", so that's my last night sleeping on the floor.

# REDEEM YOURSELF

The furniture arrived as scheduled; so I assembled the bed and put the kitchen table in the dining area. The new furniture made it feel like home, so the apartment's empty echo no longer existed. My bachelor's crib is nearly complete, besides a few more things; it would be fit for a king.

Otto is from Germany and spoke with an accent. He worked for the company as a maintenance supervisor. Otto believes in speaking his mind. He refuses to follow his supervisor's instruction and will respond to the boss' in an unprofessional manner.

The employer primarily hired me to paint, because Otto did not paint, and I had experience painting. The boss gave me other work assignments, such as electrical, plumbing and carpentry. I had no idea they were considering me for Otto's position.

Charles and I would spend hours at 2230 fellowship. Meetings were held all week and social events during the weekends. We spoke on various topics, such as addiction, sports, education, relationship and etc. The meetings allowed me to get things off my chest. People would vent their anger, frustration and whatever is on their minds.

One night, I had a nightmare and awoke in a cold sweat. The dream consisted of violence and using drugs. I dream about people that I'd harmed and having a bowl of cocaine in the refrigerator. The dream appeared to be real.

# HOW IT BEGAN

My sponsor and I discussed the dream; he gave me advice and said to make a meeting.

Shooting pool is a fun game to play. The balls are gathered in a rack, all except the cue ball; it's used to break the balls. You take the pool stick in hand, position the cue ball and proceed to play. Then decide if you have hi or low balls. Players will decide what games to play, eight ball, nine ball or calling pockets. You size up the shot, by positioning the cue ball for the next shoot.

Dancing is a form of exercise; it keeps the body in shape, and releases any frustration. I'll dance until the wee hours of the night, my clothes drenched in sweat. I enjoy playing card games, such as spades and bid wiz. Playing cards can be good for the mind, it keeps the mind sharp. These were activities that kept me sober, besides just making meetings and not getting high.

I am grateful for Alcoholic Anonymous and the people who attend meetings. People that have back grounds similar to me and that I am able to identify. You will find the answer in A.A., so the only stupid question is the one you did not ask. Intelligent people, from all walks of life, surround you.

We ought to keep gratitude in our attitude, or you will pick up. This profound statement has kept me sober throughout the years. Having gratitude has allowed me to be grateful to God; he has carried me throughout life's journey.

# REDEEM YOURSELF

It is not my power alone that has kept me sober. I've experienced some rough mountains in sobriety, and I continue to keep the faith. Each day I thank God for his blessing and giving me another chance in life.

As I continue this journey of sobriety, I began to get honest, and to accept my mistakes. I stopped blaming people, the system, or living in the ghetto. In life, I chose to become a dope fiend, because I didn't confront situations, or take responsibility for my own actions.

It has been a few months since I began working. It's a good feeling to have a job and receive a regular paycheck. Having a job brings independence and self respect. People will respect you, because you're respecting yourself. Various institutions such as banks and credit unions will loan you money.

You could now pay the rent, utility bills and buy groceries. Paying rent for some people can be difficult, for years you might've been unmanageable, but in time you learn the importance of paying rent. Paying rent is important, because it will provide you shelter, and a place to enjoy.

Friday afternoon and I am anxious to get off work, and start the weekend. I have been looking forward to the weekend, to go out and party. My immediate supervisor approaches me, saying he needs to talk with me.

# HOW IT BEGAN

So, I'm a little nervous, because I had no idea what to expect, I followed Nick into the office.

Upon entering the office, I'm instructed to have a seat. Nick's supervisor Marge is also present; they began complimenting me on a job well done. So, I realize that nothing is wrong, as I continued to listen. The supervisors offered me a promotion, to become the maintenance supervisor. Certainly I am surprise and in a state of disbelief.

The employer has terminated Otto, for not following orders, and being disrespectful towards authority. For a moment I am bewildered, so I'm having doubts about accepting the position. No experience being a supervisor and limited knowledge doing maintenance. Quietly! I recited the Serenity Prayer, and began to feel a side of relief, also a desire to accept the challenge.

You got the job! Congratulate yourself on your own abilities, qualities, and efforts that have ensured that you got the position. When good things happen, believe that good things will continue to happen. Believe that when a positive event occurs, that other positive events will occur. If you are positive, then you will see your life in a positive light, and your outlook on life will become much more positive.

So where do you start? Start by taking a personal inventory of all things you bring to the table like: the things you're good at, personal character traits, such as being hard working, resourceful, a quick learner, trustworthy and reliable, any special skills or expertise you have, knowledge you've acquired that can further the company's mission, problems you've solved; and projects you've worked on. Do a thorough inventory of yourself and figure out what you bring to the table.

"You have the weekend to consider our offer." I immediately gave the supervisors my decision. Yes! I will accept the position. As I exit the office and proceeded downstairs to the shop, I am surprise to see Otto.

He is packing his belongings. For a moment I felt sorry for him, but then realize he brought this on himself. Otto has been warned repeatedly, but he refused to listen. I said farewell and wish him good luck.

During the train ride home I thought about the promotion. This proves what hard work can do. The promotion improved my self esteem, and encouraged me to further succeed. I am able to resign from the part time job; so in order to work full time, to receive better benefits and pay.

Achievement has a tremendous amount to do with feelings and emotions. If you want to accomplish something badly enough, then your feelings and emotions will undoubtedly help you to remain motivated until you successfully carry it through.

# HOW IT BEGAN

Every effort that you make towards the things, you want in life is like making a deposit in your success account. Over the time no matter how small your efforts, your account will begin to pay interest in the form of a completed task, or an achieved goal.

For years successful men and women have understood the phase every step counts. These three simple words pack a lot of power. Every step that you take in the direction of your plans has an accumulative effect towards the achievement of your goals. The longer you work at it and the more effort you put in, the greater your chances of accomplishing your goals.

The problem with most people is not that they don't have the skill or talent. It's that they don't have staying power. They give up too quickly and throw in the towel at the first sign of a struggle.

If you are in a situation where the pressure's on and you're ready to throw in the towel, talk to level – headed men who can tell you what to do, to keep yourself and your family together. Don't be embarrassed about letting other men, especially older wiser men; they know what's really going on.

Chances are, they have been where you are now and they'll be able to give you some feedback to better navigate the situation. Going to other men for counsel is not a sign of weakness. It's a sign of maturity.

# REDEEM YOURSELF

Nobody has all the answers all the time. Not even you. It is through sharing your experiences and learning from the experiences of others that you become wiser and grow. Even more, you'll get the resources and answers you need to sustain yourself and your family.

# ATTITUDE

You must have a burning desire to achieve a particular goal. Unless you have the desire, you will most probably find it difficult to achieve what you set out to do. Failure to succeed is more likely due to a lack of desire rather than any obstacles in your way.

While eating breakfast a feeling of gratitude came over me, being grateful for my parent's teaching. Mama explained the importance of knowing how to cook. If you're married and the wife is sick, you could feed your family. Restaurants will be too expensive, but being able to cook is a plus. It was interesting watching both parents in the kitchen cooking.

# REDEEM YOURSELF

My thoughts were suddenly interrupted by the sound of the doorbell ringing. The furniture has been delivered. After arranging the living room furniture, I stepped back to admire the crib. The telephone has already been installed. It brought me great satisfaction to observe this accomplishment. And I began to feel right at home.

Monday morning and I'm reporting to work, but within a different job capacity. Being a maintenance supervisor will require much responsibility. The position will not be easy but I am up for the challenge. Three employees will report to me, two maintenance workers and one housekeeper.

I met with the employees to discuss certain matters. They were working for the company longer than me. An employee asked me, why he did not get the position? "Nick should've asked me." "You need to address your concern with Nick."

Maria and I worked for the same company. She is married with children, but not happily married. She would discuss her situations at home, so I would listen with an attentive ear, and give her a shoulder to cry on. She would sometimes bring me home cook meals for lunch. It might've been left over food, but she certainly can cook.

My first year being sober and I am grateful to God. For I reflect on the year's accomplishments: graduating from Anchor House and receiving a certificate.

# ATTITUDE

The employer has given me a promotion and a substantial pay increase. My apartment is completely furnished.

This first anniversary is not a graduation, so I have to continue making meetings and not pick up. I am told the first year is a gift, but did not understand the terminology. So, I'll continue carrying the message to those still suffering. Attending meetings are people life line.

People will celebrate years of sobriety without alcohol or drugs, and this is considered a great achievement. It shows how far you've come in sobriety, facing obstacles, doubts and fears. And each year is a new beginning to grow and to further progress.

Maria and I decided to host a Thanksgiving dinner; we will invite family and friends. Our children will be meeting for the first time. We decided on a few different meals. Our relationship is no longer a secret, her family and I enjoyed each other company.

Maria is a beautiful woman and she has good qualities. I am ready to take our relationship to another level. She wanted more time to consider a divorce. She admitted to no longer loving her husband, but need to consider her children. "Hope she makes a decision soon."

The job presented a challenge, due to emergency and decisions having to be made.

# REDEEM YOURSELF

Often times, I'm learning to "think on my feet," in order to resolve an emergency. Learn to do repair and inventory. After three months the boss congratulates me, and tells me I'm doing a good job. And I'm given a salary increase.

Maria came by the crib after work. She often spends the weekend and return home on Sunday. We'd have a wonderful time socializing and doing things with the children. Our relationship is getting serious, so at times it did not matter if she's married.

She arrived at the crib, and gets comfortable, but appeared to be avoiding me. I feel if though something is wrong. Maria! Is everything all right? She replied that everything is okay; I did not get that impression. She still was wearing sun glasses in the crib. Being suspicious I believe that something is wrong.

Her back is turn towards me, as she avoids eye contact. Turn her around towards me, and remove the sun glasses. I am shocked to see her with a black eye. She told me her husband done it. Why? "I told him about you."

"Did he say something to upset you?" Yeah! "He said something that made me angry, so I told him about you, and he proceeded punching me." Surely after several months, he should've recognized a difference in you.

30

# ATTITUDE

Maria's husband hitting her disturbed me; it put me at a disadvantage, my hands were tied. This man is her husband, so I could not confront him, and therefore not much I could've done. Maria is not my wife to protect, but still I care about her. She insists on seeing me regardless of her husband's physical abuse.

Domestic violence hurts all family members. When a person is abusive he or she eventually loses the trust and respect of his or her partner. Abused partners are afraid to communicate their feelings and needs.

Domestic violence is a serious problem. It is a common cause of injury. Victims may suffer physical injuries, such as bruises or broken bones. They may suffer emotionally from depression, anxiety or social isolation.

Domestic violence is a violent confrontation between family or household members involving physical harm, or fear of physical harm. Household family include spouses/former spouses, those in (or formerly in) a dating relationship, adults by blood or marriage, and those who have biological or legal parent – child relationship.

It is hard to know exactly how common domestic violence is, because people often do not report it. There is no typical victim. It happens among people of all ages. It affects those of all levels of income and education.

# REDEEM YOURSELF

When you change your old ways, your attitude also changes. The old negative me would've done some - thing; because of my pride and being macho. I would not have thought about the consequences, such as someone being hurt or the possibility of going to prison, and the children are possible without a dad.

The actions we take in life, if it's good or bad has a price. You will pay a consequence for every negative decision made in life. Let's say I'd taken a negative course of action. Now I stand before a judge to answer the charges(s). What do I say in my defense?

Some people go through their whole life, never taken responsibility for the choices they make in life. They overstep the appropriate boundary. Act with hostile intent. Refuse to abide by the law. Inflict pain and misery on others. Then deny any wrong doing on their part when it's time to face the consequences of their action.

The job continues to be a challenge, but indeed very rewarding. The workers were on point and did their job. The job is paying a decent salary and I'm able to pay the rent, utilities and buy groceries.

A doctor examined me; he did not believe my injury is serious. Unable to turn my head is a serious matter. He was not concerned about my health, he appears interested in my health insurance and if he would get paid. You rest the weekend and return to work on Monday.

32

# ATTITUDE

In my present situation I will seek a second doctor's opinion. I located a doctor in Crown Heights; she examines me, asked questions, and did a thorough exam. "Have you fallen lately or hit your head?" No, nothing like that has happen, but she insisted some - thing has happened. Suddenly I remembered; a year prior, I had fallen off a ladder and hit my head.

"You are having a delayed reaction from the fall. Your condition is considered a whiplash." She placed a neck brace around my neck. "You are not to go to work, stay home and rest. I will see you next week to begin therapy."

I contacted the supervisor by telephone, and explain my condition. One week later, I stopped by the job, to inform Nick about my condition, and tell him I'm going on disability. To my surprise he presented me with a memo. The memo states I abandoned my job and accused for not notifying the employer. For a moment I stood there in total disbelief, I could not believe this is happening, but I will not allow their action to get me down. Repeated the serenity prayer and walk out the office.

The employer's action did not surprise me, because they are known for denying employees unemployment. In the mean time I will continue treatment, and collecting disability.

# REDEEM YOURSELF

Maria and I went grocery shopping, because Thanksgiving is quickly approaching, we want to avoid the crowd. The children were excited and looking forward to Thanksgiving. We will cook a large dinner. My son's are spending the holiday with their dad.

It has been two months since the injury, so I continued seeing the doctor, and receiving physical therapy. Being on the machine is soothing, so I look forward to the treatment, also my health is improving. Often times I'll fall asleep on the machine. Doctor! You are responding well to treatment.

Stop by the job to take Maria to lunch; she is surprised to see me. My co workers are happy to see me. "Jerome! How are you doing and when are you returning to work?" I'm feeling much better but not certain when I'll return. A few employees tell me my legal rights.

Maria and I enjoyed lunch and shared a few laughs. Her children were doing well and looking forward to seeing me. "They are anxious to meet your son's and they are looking forward to Thanksgiving. I will begin cooking Wednesday." "Maria! I enjoyed you treating me to lunch." She then kiss me good bye.

Wednesday morning and I began preparing the food. I will be cooking late into the night. My son's are ringing the door bell; they have arrived early. Dad! "We want to help cook."

# ATTITUDE

I assigned each one a different task and we worked as a team."

"Troy! Mama wants you to send her a plate. Yvonne appears to have a change of heart, she's allowing the children to visit and spend the holiday with me. I'm uncertain about her motives, so I'm certain she has a plain, but I will just enjoy the moment."

Maria and her children arrived early Thanksgiving morning. Our children were introduced to one another. It's amazing that our children are all males. The children began playing and having a terrific time. They appear to connect just fine. Maria takes over the cooking while I relaxed.

A few guests have just arrived; it is wonderful to see family and friends. Later, we gathered around the table, to give God thanks for everything. As a child I look forward to Thanksgiving, we celebrated with family, and always a joyous occasion in our home.

This holiday we referred to as Thanksgiving is no longer a tradition, it has become insignificant. Society does not recognize Thanksgiving, as a day of rejoicing and given God praise. This economy makes it difficult for many families to celebrate the holiday(s), due to people being out of work and losing their homes.

Two weeks before Thanksgiving, you will see Christmas decorations going up and hear talk of Christmas sales.

# REDEEM YOURSELF

Many people do not recognize the significance of Christmas; it represents the birth of Jesus.

People who cannot afford to purchase gifts; they will find a way to buy gifts, such as videos, iPods, etc. Even though they cannot pay their rent, or face being in debt the beginning of the New Year.

Everyone is eating and enjoying themselves. "Maria! Looks at the children, they are playing well together." Our relationship appears to be serious, so I'll see what the future holds; but I will not count on it. Uncle Clarence was enjoying Maria's sister company; she's flirting with him and he is enjoying it.

Even though It's the start of a new year, I have not made any resolution. But I hope this will be a good year. Maria's oldest son called me. "Jerome! We need to talk." "Okay! What is on your mind?" "I'm afraid for my mother's safety, because my dad has threatened her with a knife, and I believe he may hurt her."

This child's concerns could not be taken lightly, because this is a serious matter and needs to be address. "Maria! It is important that we talk. "She came by the crib, as though nothing has happened. But I expected that she sensed something is wrong. "Why did your husband threaten you with a knife?"

One national study reported that the ratio to child violence was 114 percent greater in Black families than in White families.

# ATTITUDE

"Many children in abusive households go on to become violent abusers themselves. Countless others will simple never learn how to become responsible, loving parents. The cycle of abuse and neglect will send child welfare and self – esteem issues into an entire generation of American Blacks.

Domestic violence and abuse can happen to anyone, yet the problem is often overlooked, excused, or denied. This is especially true when the abuse is psychological, rather than physical. Emotional abuse is often minimized, yet it can leave deep and lasting scars.

Domestic violence and abuse are used for one purpose and one purpose only: to gain and maintain total control over you. An abuser doesn't "play fair." Abusers use fear, guilt, shame, and intimidation to wear you down and keep you under their thumb. Your abuser may also threaten you, or hurt those around you.

Statistics from the Domestic Violence resource center: One in four women (25%) will experience domestic violence in her life time. More than three women and one man are murdered by their intimate partners in the United States every day.

Your abuser's apologies and loving gestures in between the episodes of abuse can make it difficult to leave.

# REDEEM YOURSELF

He may make you believe that you are the only person for him, that things will be different this time, and that he truly loves you. However, the dangers of staying are very real.

"We have been seeing each other for awhile, so I have feelings for her, but it's time to make a decision. Maria! You must decide between your husband and me." She did not want to choose between us. "Your safety and the children's safety are of concern. If something were to happen, I could never forgive myself. Our relationship is over; we need to go our separate ways."

One day, I'm standing on the side walk talking with friends. Tommy and Manual yells good morning to this woman exiting the building. The woman smiles in our direction. She has the most beautiful smile, I have ever seen. So, I had to meet this woman, so I ran down the block towards her, yelling for her to wait.

As I approached her, she has a look of concern, as she continues staring at me. I'm catching my breath as I tell her my name. She tells me her name is Patricia. She is trying to imagine what is going on. She noticed me wearing a neck brace. "Oh! These injuries happen on the job.

Patricia! Are you going to invite me upstairs? She politely tells me no, and proceeded across the street. So, I stand there watching as she entered the store.

# ATTITUDE

Tommy and Manual spoke highly of Patricia; they too show an interest in her. She has recently moved to the projects and basically keeps to herself. She appeared to be a woman of good qualities.

Spending hours talking with the guys; we're having a meeting of the minds. Patricia came walking out the building and again I approached her. "Are you going to the store?" Yeah! "Could I help carry your bags?" "No thank you, I could manage." A few minutes later, she walked out the supermarket carrying groceries.

As she walks towards the building, she appeared surprise to see me. "I'll open the door for you." Once inside the building, I continue rapping. She is adamant in her decision, and would not invite me upstairs. "You are a very determine young man!" Yeah! "I'll tell you what, here is my phone number, and you can take me out to dinner." While entering the elevator, she realizes I am watching her and she begins to smile.

"Uncle Clarence! I'm buying a car." So, he made an offer to give me his car. He owed traffic tickets and did not want his vehicle confiscated. So, I took a moment to consider his offer. Having a few thousand dollars to purchase a car, I instead accepted his offer.

"Patricia! Would you like to go for a drive, to get the car inspected?" Yeah! "After the car inspection, we will drive to Coney Island." "Okay! Give me a minute to change clothes."

# REDEEM YOURSELF

During the drive I happen to notice Patricia's legs; so my eyes were not on the road, and therefore I did not notice the red light. A police officer yelled for me to stop and gave me a ticket.

After the car inspection we proceeded to Coney Island, and went directly to Nathans. We order franks, frog legs and claims. After eating we went on the rides and later walk on the boardwalk. We are holding hands and sharing conversation, also observing the scenery. We are enjoying each other's company.

The doctor said my rehabilitation has gone well, and that I can return to work. The employers would not allow me to return to work. They even decided not to give me unemployment, so this is a matter of concern, and need to be heard in court.

The employer arrived in court ready to deny me unemployment. Nick walk over to me; how are you doing? "Is everything alright?" Yeah! The court officer calls our names; we proceed in the court room and seated at a table. Moments later, we are ask to stand, as the judge entered the room. Raise your right hand to be sworn in. You promise to tell the whole truth and nothing but the truth, so help you God. The burden of proof lies upon the employer.

The judge asks the employer to present their case. Two supervisors explain their position with the company.

# ATTITUDE

"Jerome! Abandon his job and has excessive absences." Therefore we had no chose but to terminate his employment.

It's time to present my case; I explain the importance of my position as a supervisor. I presented several doctor's notes explaining the absences. Judge! The employer gave me a memo several months ago; it stated that I had called the supervisor, and came into the office explaining my condition.

Judge! Made inquiries about the memo given me. The employer appeared surprise when I presented the memo. How did the employee abandon his job? You stated he did not contact you. The memo states an entirely different story. Judge! The employee is entitled to collect unemployment.

This had been a triumphant moment, because I stood up for my rights and the truth was revealed. The truth outweights the supervisors plot. Being triumphant is a fantastic feeling. This victory will motivate me, to face other obstacles in life. People should stand up for their rights.

Today, there is simply too much behavior that is regarded as "acceptable", and respect for many values has rapidly diminished. You have the choice to live your own life.

# REDEEM YOURSELF

Stand up for what you believe in, if you really want to succeed, adhere to the rules and values that are important to you. Do not let others persuade you to accept anything less than your own high standards. Aim high as far as your standards and principles are concerned. Believe in your own high standard, and you will achieve much in life.

Patricia and I are going steady, and we are often together. She is a fantastic cook and knows her way around the kitchen. She knows the way to a man's heart is through his stomach. We enjoy various activities, such as going to the amusement park, the movies and on picnics. We'd often go places with friends.

"Patricia! Will you live with me?" Yeah! You must first ask my mother. "I am not proposing marriage." "It does not matter; you should speak with my mother. "Why should I ask your mother, if you could live with me?" "In order to know what type of man you are." That afternoon I paid her mother a visit.

Mama! "We need to talk! Can your daughter come live with me?" "It's okay but under one condition. You promise to take care of my daughter." Mama! "I promise to take care of her." She gave me her blessing, as if though we were getting married.

Patricia and I were now in a relationship; no longer could I consider myself a bachelor.

# ATTITUDE

It is time I began to settle down. Being single is fun, but now the thrill is gone. Our relationship is the start of something positive.

Collecting unemployment is not enough money, so I needed a hustle, but first allow me to elaborate. I speak about a change and doing positive things in life. The hustling I speak about is not a criminal act, such as stealing, or selling drugs. In my memoir "Lust of a Dope Fiend" it speaks about hustling.

There are different types of hustling within the system. Having a job will provide you an income. Learn the stock market or invest in real estate, also think long term investment. Become an entrepreneur and operate your own business. So, I decided to paint people's homes.

I received unfortunate news that my cousin Gerald died; his death came as no surprise, since he had been sick. Gerald is a few years older than me. He was a smooth conservative person.

Are people ever truly ready, for times such as death? The church is jammed pack and people were standing in the aisles and outside the church. He has left his mark in life, because he has touched the lives of many people.

Two weeks after Gerald's death, Uncle Elijah died from cancer. He had been in and out the Veteran's Hospital.

# REDEEM YOURSELF

He was generally a quiet person who enjoyed the simple things in life. He is one of my favorite uncles, I enjoyed his company.

Aunt Mary his wife treated Elijah like a king. She was my aunt by marriage and treated me better than family. Aunt Mary was there for me, in good and bad times. It is time for me to stand by her side and be a pillar of support.

Concerning these deaths I begin to question God. Who am I to question God? The Bible says death is promise to us all. These deaths were disturbing and I always consider myself strong, but these deaths had bewildered me. Just like my mother's death was extremely difficult; her death had taken me over the edge, and into a life of despair.

We all get to a point that dealing with situation(s) can feel overwhelming, or possible lose hope and cannot see our way out. We have all been there, even the people who look like they have it together. It could be money troubles, a broken heart, and an unforeseen illness, the death of a love one, or loneliness and growing frustration with life. We get to a point where we get desperate and contemplate doing something rash.

But no matter how bad things appear to be, right now, as long as you've got breath in your body you have an opportunity to make a fresh start.

# ATTITUDE

It may take you a minute or two to see your way clearly, but as long as you are alive you have the ability to change your life for the better.

It's easy to get discourage when the storms of life wear on you. It's even easier to give up on yourself and the ones you love when the storms of life affect your ability to provide. But it is during these times that you must hold on to the notion that you are needed and necessary no matter what's going on around you or what you've lost.

To fully experience joy and happiness, we accepted that we must also experience adversity and trails in our lives. We were promised however, that our trails would never be so terrible that we could not endure them. Once we have lived a fruitful and productive life on earth, death will mark the start of our journey home to live with God.

My unemployment checks were about to end. So, I begin to network and searching for a job. Joe gave me a call and asks whether I'll be interested in a job. Without any hesitation I said okay. He set a date and time to be interviewed.

Joe and I met in the early eighties, we had much in common. Joe was a supervisor at a University and worked in the computer department. He explained the clerk position and saved the best for last. Salary! I'm not completely satisfied with the salary but realize something is better than nothing.

# REDEEM YOURSELF

With more and more people looking for work these days, you cannot afford to be left behind in the marketplace. In order to find a decent paying job and remain gainfully employed you've got to be employable and know what kind of work situations you best thrive in. Even more, you've got to transfer your strengths into marketable skills and attributes that add value to the workforce.

So many people expect to begin at the top and not climb the ladder to success. People should learn to crawl before they walk. Often people find it difficult to swallow their pride. Pride will not feed you or your family, or provide you shelter. First! You get your feet in the door, be motivated to work hard and better opportunities will occur.

"Joe! I will accept the position and keep our relationship professional. When do I start working?" "Could you start next week?" Yeah! "I'm elated you considered me for the position." I meet Patricia at her mother's crib; she is excited to hear the good news.

One night lying awake in bed, I began thinking about my sons, and the decision I'm about to make. Patricia happened to notice me shedding tears, because I had decided to remove myself from the children's life. It was not an easy decision, but I had enough of Yvonne's unnecessary nonsense.

# ATTITUDE

Taken Yvonne to court was a waste of time; she refused to honor the judge's decision and continued using the children against me. Dealing with her aggression had become overwhelming and therefore I had to consider my sanity. So, I continued supporting the children.

There are mothers of children without fathers in the home, who take advantage of the fact that they have ultimate control of when the fathers that want to do the right thing, see their children and how money they are given is spent on their children. They are violent vengeful women who cannot deal with the fact. They are not number one anymore and make visitation difficult. The children suffer no matter the situation.

Joe approached me on the job. Let's talk about a promotion. "What type of promotion?" "It's a computer technician position." Yeah! "It will be on the job training and more money." I am excited by the news and ready to accept the position.

A few months later, Joe approaches me with bad news. "We are being laid off the job." Joe being laid off came as a shock; because of his commitment and years of service. So, I will be collecting unemployment and seeking another job.

Not long after being laid off, I'm in a car accident and my car is totaled. The driver roared through the red light and hit the car with such an impact.

# REDEEM YOURSELF

He approached the car and stuck his head inside the window. Sir! "Are you okay?" His breath smelled of alcohol. I was slightly dazed but fully aware of my surroundings. The ambulance attendant removed me from the wreck and is taken me to the hospital.

Patricia is sitting on the bench, and happens to notice the car being towed. She began worrying about me. And she went to two different hospitals searching for me. Upon entering the emergency room, she has a look of concern.

The nurse pointed her in my direction. She quickly approaches me, asking, are you alright? Yeah! "Seeing the condition of the car had me worried. I am happy to see that you are okay." Patricia being concerned got me to thinking. We have been together a few years; she has been there for me in good and bad times.

It is time I proposed marriage; she would be in shock. She is not aware that I will ask her to marry me. "Patricia! We need to talk." "Is everything okay Yeah! "What is on your mind?" "Will you marry me?" She appeared to be in a daze.

She ask me to come into the bedroom; she sat down on the bed. "Will you repeat the question?" She has wanted to get married for awhile; she could not believe her ears. I knelt on one knee, placing her hand in my hand. Baby! "Will you marry me?" "Yes!!!" We decided to discuss the wedding plans, at a later time.

# ATTITUDE

I look forward to getting married; because its time I settle down and be committed to one woman. Having matured in areas of my life, and stop being so macho, has got me to this point. It is certainly a big step in our life, we are indeed excited.

Within three months, another situation has occurred, beside the job laying me off, and the car being totaled, my brother Gilbert unexpected death. Dad's health will not allow him to make funeral arrangements, so therefore I made the necessary arrangements. I'd gone to the morgue to identify the body.

I am directed into a room. A few minutes later the curtains open and there lay my brother's body. "Sir! Is this your brother?" "Yes! That is my Brother." The curtain is immediately drawn close. I sign a form to release his body to the mortician, and I proceeded to the funeral parlor to make the necessary arrangements.

Gilbert and I we're very close growing up: he meant the world to me. He was much different than me; we were different as night and day. He had a good heart, a humble spirit, and willing to help people.

Someone from the funeral office call me, to check out the body. He is done to my specification, so I am satisfied and the funeral will proceed as scheduled. My brother lay there in the coffin; so I recalled when we were children, playing with toys, riding our bikes, and having fun.

# REDEEM YOURSELF

This is indeed a strange experience; it's like watching a movie projector playing back in time.

People attend his funeral to pay their respect. Several people said kind words regarding my brother. On a sunny day, I visited Gilbert in Queens. He spoke about me being sober, and my positive attitude. His words truly inspired me.

As the service came to a close, we were instructed to proceed to New Jersey. As we stood around the grave, the sun is beaming down on us. The Pastor said a prayer, as the body is being lowered in the ground. My last words "Brother, rest in peace."

Those few months prior have been rough and sobriety has not been an easy journey, but I'm committed to staying sober. My sobriety is built on a solid foundation. Certainly I would have some rough mountains to climb and situations to endure. Question! Could I remain sober under any condition?

Sometime ago I made a decision to seek quality sobriety. I know people who have years of quantity sobriety, but had no strong foundation and therefore unable to handle situation. People still holding on to old ideas and are not willing to accept change. They continue to scheme on the system, or do nothing constructive in their life. Having quality sobriety helps you face obstacle(s) and overcome various situations.

# ATTITUDE

Ernest confronted me after the meeting. Sponsor! "How are you doing?" "Okay!" "I need to ask you a question?" Yeah! "Lately you have experience a few situations, such as your brother's death, losing a job and your car. With all that has happened, how do you remain positive?"

You learn to stay sober under any situation. We ought to build a strong foundation and be honest with ourselves. Repeating the serenity prayer has given me the courage and strength to get through these rough times. So, I suggest that you learn the serenity prayer and apply it to your life.

Upon entering Alcoholic Anonymous I had no job or car. I will continue to stay sober and get a better job, a new car. My brother will always remain in my heart. Whatever happens in life, I have made a conscious decision to stay sober, and rely on a higher power.

## A CHANGE

You should cherish your gratitude and be grateful to be alive. This profound statement has kept me sober throughout the years. Having gratitude has allowed me to be grateful to God, he has carried me throughout life's journey, and it was not my power alone that's kept me sober. I have endured some rough mountains to climb in sobriety and I will continue to have faith.

Alcoholic Anonymous has allowed me to build a strong foundation; the twelve steps provide me structure. The greatest power I have today is a Choice. A choice to say yes to that is (good) for me and (no) to that is bad for me. I confront situation(s) in life differently. Having a strong foundation is indeed vital, in order to overcome situation(s).

# REDEEM YOURSELF

Come unto me, all ye that labor and are heavy laden, and I will give you rest.

Matthews 11:28

For those in treatment for alcohol or drugs, the twelve steps are used to guide an addicted person toward freedom of abstinent. You admit being powerless over your addiction, you believe that a power greater than yourself could restore you to sanity.

There are millions in Alcoholic Anonymous, Narcotic Anonymous, self-help programs, and graduates from residential treatment facilities who have been clean and sober for years. They will tell you that they did not do it alone, and that there were steps they had to take, to get to the point in life where they wanted to live.

All State Insurance appeared in Small Claims Court; refusing to pay for my car damages. During the hearing they claimed I cause the accident, and therefore they were not being held responsible. I presented pictures to the judge; it showed car damages and pictures do not lie.

My car sustained no damage in the front. How could I cause the accident? The car has been totaled and beyond repair, also the ambulance drove me to the hospital. The judge awarded me the decision in the case.

# A CHANGE

The attorney is not pleased about the judge's decision; he believes I should not receive book value or any extra money. Judge! The car had a sentimental value to the plaintiff; he invested money and time into the car. The car means more to him, then the book value. Judge! "My decision for the plaintiff's is final."

In the early 1980s I began working with the homeless population; we go around the city helping people in distress. Driving around the city was indeed a job; your eyes would have to be on the road. The social workers and I would meet people on the street or inside the van, offering food, or places to get shelter, also help people receive benefits.

Many homeless people prefer to live on the streets, because they fear for their safety living in shelters; violence is inflicted upon them and their property stolen.

This is indeed an interesting job; I met people from all walks of life, people of different nationalities, speaking various languages and some holding professional positions. People arrive in New York from different countries and states.

Working with homeless people has been a rewarding experience. And I'm reminded that I am grateful. So many different stories have been told, people losing their job, evicted from their homes, getting divorce, dealing with a spouse's death.

# REDEEM YOURSELF

I am able to identify with being homeless, because I experienced this unpleasant situation and endure people's humiliation. That experience helps me to keep it real. We should never take life for granted, because you may be up today and down tomorrow. Yes! It could happen to you, or your family and friend(s).

About 3.5 million U.S. residents, including children have been homeless for a significant period of time. Domestic abuse is another cause of homelessness. According to the Ford Foundation, and 50 percent of all homeless women and children were victims of physical or other abuse by their own family.

Being homeless is very degrading to anyone. Family members and friends may turn against you, as if though you've gone into exile. People can be cruel and show no mercy. Why! They have an education, a good paying job, health, and shelter. People may believe they will never become homeless.

Two trends are largely responsible for the rise in homelessness over the past 15 - 20 years; a growing shortage of affordable rental housing and a simultaneous increase in poverty. Poor people are frequently unable to pay for housing, food, childcare, health care, and education.

Difficult choices must be made when limited resources cover only some of these necessities. Often it is housing, which absorbs a high proportion of income that must be dropped.

# A CHANGE

Being poor mean being an illness, an accident, or a paycheck away from living on the streets.

How will you respond to an unfortunate situation? Do not say it will never happen, because you are just one paycheck from being homeless. The employer only knows his employee by number; your name is not of importance. If employees can no longer perform their job, the employer will terminate the employee.

People were once productive citizens, who had jobs and a place to live. People are suffering from low self-esteem and are ashamed of their situation, but they are trying to survive in spite of their circumstances.

Racism is a series of structures that effects persons of color disproportionately with the burden of the work of living and excludes those same persons disproportionately from the benefits of their work and accomplishments. We cannot pretend this is not happening.

The National Urban league's 2009 State Black America report notes that African Americans remain twice as likely as Whites to be unemployed, three times more likely to live in poverty and more than six times as likely to be incarcerated.

These statistics tell us something about the results of our ability as a society to produce "common wealth" and prosperity for all.

# REDEEM YOURSELF

The combination of race and income in housing segregation isolates many persons of color from quality services (health care, employment and education).

Two factors help account for increasing poverty: eroding employment opportunities for large segments of the workforce, and the declining values and availability of public assistance. Thus, most states have not replaced the old welfare system with an alternative that enables families and individuals to obtain above-poverty employment and to sustain themselves when work is not available or possible.

The lack of affordable housing has led to high rent burdens (rent which absorbs a high proportion of income), overcrowding and substandard housing. These phenomena in turn, have not only force many of people to become homeless, but they have put a large and growing number of people at risk of becoming homeless.

Rent regulation provides neighborhood stability and prevents displacement, strengthening social ties in neighborhoods and ensuring that tenants can share in the benefits when their neighborhoods improve.

The Repeal vacancy Decontrol Bill will reinstate rent regulation so there will no longer be high rent increases. Rent Stabilization Protections for former Mitchell – Lama and Section 8 tenants will prevent landlords from seeking rent increases for "unique or peculiar circumstances."

# A CHANGE

"Criminalization Measures are bad Policy and Violate Constitutional Rights." Criminalization measures also raise constitutional questions and many of them violate the civil rights of homeless people. Courts have found certain criminalization measures unconstitutional.

These practices that criminalize homelessness do nothing to address the underlying causes of homelessness. Instead, they exacerbate the problem. They frequently move people away from services.

For example, when a city passes a law that places too many restrictions on begging, free speech concerns are raised as courts have found begging to be protected speech under the First Amendment.

When homeless persons are arrested and charged under these measures, they develop a criminal record, making it difficult to obtain employment or housing. Furthermore, criminalization measures are not cost efficient. In a nine city survey of supportive housing and jail costs, jail costs were on average two to three times the cost of supportive housing.

When a city destroys homeless persons' belongings or conducts unreasonable searches or seizures of homeless persons, courts have found such actions violate the Fourth Amendment right to be free from unreasonable searches and seizures.

# REDEEM YOURSELF

Courts have found that a law that is applied to criminally punish a homeless person for necessary life activities in public, like sleeping, violated that person's Eight Amendment right, to be free from cruel and unusual punishment if the person has nowhere else to perform the activity.

An unfortunate trend in cities around the country over the past twenty five years has been to turn to the criminal justice system to respond to people living in public spaces. This trend includes measures that target homeless persons by making it legal to perform life sustaining activities in public. These measures prohibit activities such as sleeping/camping, eating, sitting, and begging in public spaces, usually including criminal penalties for violation of these laws.

So many people today experience challenges they never dream existed. I call it white collar being homeless. There are people who went to college, worked hard, played by the rules, and guess what – the world changed.

Angry tenants took their frustration to the public by participating in a protest rally on July 12, 2010 to combat what they call unjust laws that diminish affordable housing for New York citizens. Tenants marched through lower Manhattan, making their frustration with the State Senate's deadlock on tenant legislation known to every pedestrian and driver in the area.

# A CHANGE

The Democratic Party had promised suffering tenants that once they seized control of the State Senate, they would undo the oppressive amendments to the rent and eviction protection laws that were imposed by the Republican majority in the last two decades. Now that time has come, yet the unjust laws are still intact.

"Democrats made promises for decades that once they took control of the State Senate, they would restore the rent Laws and reverse the damage done by Republicans who worked hard to undermine the laws when they were In power."

The Democrats have controlled the Senate for two years now, and not a single major piece of pro – tenant legislation has yet passed. A small handful of Democrats who are in the pockets of landlord lobbyists are being allowed to set the agenda, and tenants are fed up.

The Politicians and society play a major role in people's lives. They will promise people if elected jobs, housing, health care and less taxes. When they get into office, they have found excuses for not keeping promises.

Many citizens in the United States have lost confidence in the laws that are written in the United States Constitution.

# REDEEM YOURSELF

People are seeking solutions to some of the hardships they face today, while also attempting to learn about and regaining their constitutional rights. Strangely enough, we don't demand that politicians follow the laws, instead, we tend to accept their word and actions as law, and too often we seek alliance with them driven by "What in it for me?"

Who represents us is supposed to be who we elect to represent us. It is supposed to be the people's choice – one vote, one person – and in the end, political representation that represents our communities. We need a government that reflects our views, our passions, our needs, our community and our city, state and country.

Freedom to express opinions, worship or not in the religion of choice, travel from place to place within the United States, and vote for leaders of civil society are among rights that make the United States what it is. It is dangerous to assume civil and political rights are secure within the United States.

Politicians need to show us that our community is part of their agenda and that they are willing to commit themselves every day to making our communities stronger, our children better educated and our families safe and healthy.

What we are witnessing and experiencing with respect to the economic situation in America is serious.

# A CHANGE

We should not take it for granted that everything will eventually turn out alright. All we can expect from a politician is greed, exploitation, callous indifference and continued manipulation of people.

"If you fail to plan, you plan to fail." Black politicians and preachers are failing to serve and satisfy their roles as shepherds even though they are handsomely paid. They are begging for more money. Their job is to disseminate relevant information for our survival. The lack of information is the parasite of the Black Community.

We decided on a day to get married and how many guests to invite. The guest(s) list includes one hundred people. The food served will be fried chicken, roast beef, barbecue ham, various starches and vegetables. There will be enough food to serve the guest. During the months ahead we have a task to accomplish.

It is hard to believe that I'm getting married; never could I imagine being married, or settling down with someone. Is it possible I fear marriage, or being committed and having responsibility for someone? Patricia and I would soon be married, she will become my soul mate, we have so much in common.

"Patricia! We need to talk; I have something on my mind and need to discuss the matter. Have you changed your mind about getting married?" "No!" "Would a marriage license change us? Will you allow me to be myself?" Yeah!

# REDEEM YOURSELF

"I would never try to change you." Couples have been together for years, and then decide to get married, and within a year, file for a divorce.

June 25$^{th}$ has finally arrived, we were getting married. The phone is constantly ringing and people calling to congratulate us. Two ministers are called to perform the marriage, to make certain the pastor arrives on time. To my surprise, both pastors arrived on time, so I excused one pastor but he is invited to stay.

Reverend Pratt will perform the marriage; he stood before me holding the bible and patiently waiting for the bride to appear. Richard my best man is standing beside me. Richard and his wife have been married for years. In a way he's my mentor, due to his experience.

Patricia walks into the room looking gorgeous, in her beautiful wedding dress and her pretty smile. Her radiant beauty caught my attention, my eyes were fix on her; she appeared like an angel from heaven. Dad did the honors of delivering the bride to me.

We stood before the Pastor as he read a scripture from the bible. He told us to repeat after him. We repeated the vows and put the rings on each other's finger. "And with the power invested in me, I now pronounce you man and wife. You may kiss the bride"; it's a long passionate kiss as someone call time out.

# A CHANGE

The music began playing; we are the first to dance. We're dancing to a romantic song, as I whispered the melodies in her ear. People soon join us dancing. The guests were enjoying the reception. We were happy to see everyone enjoying themselves.

The wedding and reception were magnificent. People were generous with money and gifts. People of various nationalities attended the wedding and this special occasion means a lot. This marriage would not have happened, if I had not made a change in life.

Enjoy every day! Take the time to appreciate the beautiful world in which you live. Enjoy being with the people that you love, and show them that you love them. Show gratitude for everything in your life. Appreciate what you have, because these have been gifts given to you. Make the most of your talents to lead a really fulfilling and rewarding life.

## PRICE YOU PAY

In today's world raising children has drastically change, you rarely see two parents in a household. Single mothers are the head of household and raising the children alone. A home without a father is incomplete.

Dads are the male figure in a child's life; and daughters especially need their father's affection. Fathers need to be a role model and the mother's role is equally important. Children need the guidance of both parents.

My sons would spend weekends with me; they were under ten years old. Being a single dad, I never imagined what single mothers had to endure. Children are very active, curious, and they are into everything. Parents are constantly watching their children; to make sure they are safe.

# REDEEM YOURSELF

Time I spent with the children was indeed a learning experience.

Parents getting divorce can be a disaster. Parents are going to family court, in order to resolve their issue(s). Mothers having resentment towards the fathers; may not allow the children to see their father. Often mothers are angry with the children's father, so therefore they use the children like a pawn, to play against their dad.

So many children are in a state of confusion, still wondering what went wrong, how can they make it right again, who can they trust with their private thoughts and emotions. They may have doubts on getting married or becoming a parent.

There is a price you pay when you allow yourself to become bitter. That price is happiness and peace of mind, even if your anger is justified and you believe the other person has it coming. If you allow even an ounce of bitterness to get the best of you and it goes Un-checked, eventually that ounce becomes a gallon which over time grows into a cancerous tidal wave of un-controlled rage or depression, which is anger turned inward.

Yvonne happens to notice Patricia entering the car. From the looks of things, she did not appreciate it. She believes she ought to be sitting beside me. She has been trying to resume a relationship. I am willing to be her friend, but being a friend is not good enough.

# PRICE YOU PAY

She immediately became resentful and would not allow the children to visit. "Certainly you have heard that misery loves company."

"There are fathers who have been victimized by parental alienation or an overzealous mother who feels that she can dictate every dimension of the father/child relationship." Know your rights. You have the right to have family time with your children without interference from their mother. If your child's mother is denying you access to your child, get court ordered visitation. If you suspect that things will get nasty at the visits, arrange for Friday to Monday visits at a neutral pick – up and drop off point like your child's school or the child care.

I went to court and filed a petition against Yvonne, she is given a date to appear in court, because I had had enough of her nonsense, she has had her way long enough. And I am entitled to see the children. People of color crowed the court house. We will stand before a judge and he will make the decision.

We have been waiting awhile to be call, so little conversation exists between us and finally a court officer calls our name. We proceeded into the courtroom and had a seat. The judge entered the court and the court officer asks everyone to stand.

We are call to come forward, raise our right hand, To be sworn in to testify. The judge asks us questions we respond with an answer. Judge made his decision and granted me visitation rights.

# REDEEM YOURSELF

Yvonne is not satisfied with the judge's decision.

She tried to have the judge reverse his decision. The judge asked, "Is he the father of your children?" "Yes!" "Therefore I cannot deny him visitation rights; he has a right to see his children. Why would you not allow him in the children's life?" She could not answer his question.

Men handle your business; your children are your responsibility, they are entitled to financial support. We should not allow bitterness to override our judgment. Never can it be said I did not support my children.

Brother, the answer to your problems is not in the arms of another woman, a bottle of alcohol, the streets, in detaching yourself emotionally or in allowing yourself to sink into a bottomless pit of depression.

It is connection with level – headed men who can show you how to keep your head right and your family together when the storms of life rain on you and the ones you love.

Troy called me sounding upset. Dad! "You must go to court, because mom is trying to send me away, you need to stop her." Upon entering the court I noticed Yvonne sitting on the bench: she appeared surprised to see me. She had no idea our son called me.

"Yvonne! Why would you send Troy away?" he is out of control and I cannot handle him."

68

# PRICE YOU PAY

"Why not give me a call?" "You might've been busy." That is a poor excuse; I would have made time; he is our son."

An employee of the court is asking Yvonne questions. She is belligerent towards me, because it is decided that Troy would live with me. "Instead you rather have him confined." Son! You will be living with dad, because you're still a minor and I am your legal guardian.

There are so many scars inside of black men and women, that sometimes without realizing it; we tear each other down when we should be building each other up. With all that we are struggling with and against, it's no wonder that sometimes we struggle to love ourselves and each other.

Troy did not want to abide by any rules; he wants to party and do whatever. Living with his mother, he had no rules to follow or any set time to be home. "Troy! Dad will not tolerate your nonsense." He stayed a few days, but he is not satisfied with the terms and therefore he decides to leave.

An employee from the Bureau of Children Welfare (B.C.W.) visit my home, he wants to investigate me. He entered my home expressing anger, being rude and making accusations. "You will discipline your son in a certain manner."

# REDEEM YOURSELF

Sir! "You will not enter my home disrespecting me, or telling me how to raise my son. I refuse to be intimidated by you or the Bureau of Children Welfare. Your facility wants to intimidate parents and tell them how to raise their children." He received the message loud and clear and decided to act professional.

Yvonne told the man bad things about me. She insisted on living in the past, it's been difficult for her to forget. Sir! Whatever she has told you, it happens to be true. I cannot undo the past and neither will I dwell on it.

Parents believe their hands are tied and afraid the law will send them to prison. "It is hard for parents to raise their children right in a society that places special obstacles in their way." Children want to reverse the parent's role; instead they want to be the adult and the parent to be the child.

When you hold on to the issues in your life that create pain, shame and fear, you hold yourself hostage to the pain, shame and fear. This puts a block on your blessings. When the painful and shameful things in your life come to the surface, it is life's way of telling you that you are more than capable of handling the things in your life that you need to address. This enables you to move forcefully into your future.

Various agencies are the children's existing parents; theses agencies would not relinquish their authority, or allow parents to raise their children.

# PRICE YOU PAY

If you spank a child it is considered physical abuse or speak to a child in a certain manner, it is considered verbal abuse.

Children know the law better than their parents, and will threaten to report parents to the authority. Children are taught their rights in school and instructed to contact the authorities. Children will threaten their parents, so especially if she/he could not get their way, and children are not aware of the consequences.

Children are separated from their parent(s), siblings, and their friends, living in a facility among strangers, having to obey rules or else suffer the consequences. You are now in the system and going from one place to another. Parent(s) taken time off from work to appear in court, and must give an account for their action.

Granddad! "What is child abuse?" So, I explain the laws of child abuse. My grandson appears to be excited; I can imagine what he is thinking. He figures to keep his dad and grandpa in check. Grandpa! "Are you afraid of the Bureau of Children Welfare?" "No!" His smile quickly disappears; he realizes that I would not tolerate his foolishness, and would not spare the rod.

The parent who dares to discipline with the rod is one that even the toughest of street thug's secretly admires. Mama's voice and daddy's belt are still more effective than the cop's nightstick or a judge's gavel.

71

# REDEEM YOURSELF

Today, there is a continual erosion of lack of respect for those in authority. There must be more respect in the home. We must teach young and old to respect each other.

My father had several children he disciplined, and did not believe in sparing the rod/belt. He did not speak often, but I recognized the look in his eyes, and he did not hesitate chastising us. But nowadays parents are made to feel guilty, if they discipline their children.

America's weapon is the Children Services Department. Many homes are dysfunctional due to single parents and fathers not being present. Parents are afraid to discipline their children or not able to communicate with children. Parents need to raise their own children. Institutions have confiscated our children and have terminated parent's rights.

On Father's Day President Barack Obama wagged a finger at all the missing black fathers. At the Apostolic Church of God he stepped to the podium and said. "If we are honest with ourselves, we'll admit that too many fathers are missing – missing from too many lives and too many homes."

They have abandoned their responsibilities. They are acting like boys instead of men. And the foundation of our families are weaker because of it. You and I know this is true everywhere, but nowhere is this truer than in the African American Community.

# PRICE YOU PAY

Holding on to fatherhood might be a challenging task, for a father who is divorced, or not living in the home with his children, but it is not impossible. You can still hold on to your children with both hands by remaining an intricate part of your children's lives and increasing the time you spend with your children.

Here is how: First and foremost, understand your value as a father and never allow anyone to prevent you from being there for your children. Second, try not to allow personal pain to get in the way of doing what's in the best interest of your child. No matter what your relationship with your child's mother; if you hold on to fatherhood with both hands, your children will be empowered to succeed.

Strong fathers build strong communities. Over 80 percent of Black households were led by both a father and mother in the 1950s, but that number fell to less than 34 percent by 2000, according to the U.S. Census Bureau. "The breakdown of the family is caused by the absence of strong male leadership. The foundation of a strong family is built around a father's presence."

A father's absence is devastating in any community. Children without active fathers in their lives are more likely to show behavior disorders, drop out of school, run away from home, use illegal drugs and alcohol, engage in premature sex, commit violent acts, become homeless and commit suicide. A good father is a protective shield for young girls.

# REDEEM YOURSELF

Single parent(s) are working hard to support the family. Many parents are incarcerated, addicted to drugs and unable to care for their children. Children are not being taught any discipline and express little concern for human life. Children are growing up without a sense of direction.

Growing up in a world full of violence, sex, drugs, deceit and immorality and still being able to maintain your sanity may seem like a tough task for many youth. Every day we are face with peer pressure and the desire to be accepted by society and our peers as a whole.

Train up a child in the way he should go, and when he is old, he will not depart from it.

PROVERBS 22:6

The nation's education system is in a crisis. A country that once outrank the world's other industrialized nations, now trails significantly behind, as school dropout rates continue to rise and proficiency scores in the core subjects of math, reading, and science are plummeting.

Direction of Our Youth provided some shocking statistics; NYC is in the top three for the worst high school graduation rates of the nation's 50 largest school districts, with a rate of 38 percent.

# PRICE YOU PAY

In 2005, more than twenty one thousand students dropped out of NYC public high schools. There are five hundred and six failing schools in NYS, four hundred and nine of them in NYC. New York City's dropout factories (which one hundred or more students dropped out from the class of 2005) include (in Brooklyn) Lane, Adams, Madison, South Shore, FDR, Lafayette, Boys and Girls and Bushwick.

Youth are dropping out of school at an alarming rate. New York has an annual rate of twenty thousand students dropping out of school. Too many young people across the country are dropping out of school. Teenagers do not believe an education is important. What will children become without an education?

One in three U.S. high schools students drops out before graduating, more than 1.2 million students drop out every year. Statistics reveal students dropping out of school will cost the nation nearly three hundred thirty billion dollars over their life time in lost wages, taxes and productivity.

The problem is far worse for African American students, who continue to lag behind their White and Asian counterparts in achievement. As for Black males, half are expected to drop out before completing high school.

A good education in America is a major determinant of what kind of life a child will have when he or she grows up.

75

# REDEEM YOURSELF

A bad education is often a sentence to social and economic death. Education determines future income and social status as well as a child's range of future options and quality of life.

Dropping out of high school is related to a number of negative out comes. For example, the median income of persons ages 18 through 65 who had not completed high school was roughly twenty four thousand dollars in 2007.

By comparison, the median income of person's ages 18 through 65 who completed their education with a high school credential, including a General Education Development (G.E.D.) Certificate, was approximately forty thousand dollars.

Among adults ages 25 and older, a lower percentage of dropouts are in the labor force, a higher percentage of dropouts are unemployed compared with adults who earn a high school credential (U.S. Department of labor 2007). Dropouts also make up disproportionately higher percentage of the nation's prison and death row inmates.

By dropping out of school:

*You are less likely to find good jobs that pay well, bad jobs that don't pay well, or maybe any jobs.
*You are not able to afford many things you see others acquiring.

# PRICE YOU PAY

*You are more likely to get caught up in criminal activity and illegal behaviors.
*You are more likely to become involved with drugs and excessively involved with alcohol.
*You will more likely spend time in jail or prison.
*You will less like have a good, stable marriage or relationship.
*You will not have many choices where to live, your low income will require you to live in undesirable location.
*Your children will be more likely to follow in your footsteps and drop out of high school.
*You will be more likely not to vote or to lose your voting rights.

How much money do you want to make? This is what you are projected to make in your life time of working at these educational levels:

High School Dropout: $750.000
High School Diploma: $1,100.000
Bachelor's Degree: $2,100.000
Master's degree: $2,500.000
Doctorate: $4,400.000

As the world moves towards science, technology, engineering, math and medicine fewer than 50 percent of black children graduate from high school in the United States. Many of those who graduate are given diplomas that qualify them for low – wage jobs or no jobs at all, street corner hustling, incarceration and violent death.

# REDEEM YOURSELF

Teachers are finding it difficult to teach the children, because parents are not disciplining their children at home and therefore children are having behavioral problems. A teachers' job is to teach, it is not to discipline children.

Students run wild and get away with things in school that they'd normally get arrested, for a lot of bullying occurs in schools and this result in kids who are on the positive track following the negative crowd, in order to save face from a beat down.

When children and students are not cooperative, self – managed and self - disciplined, they cannot effectively learn. Teachers are being ask to be social workers, disciplinarians and police officers as well as teachers. With this expectation, there is no way that they can be successful in any of these roles, especially that of a teacher.

In many schools, the school day is spent on containment rather than enlightenment. It is no coincidence that the student populations with the highest suspension, expulsion and arrest rates have the lowest reading, math and writing scores, and lowest graduation rates.

Society needs to stop pointing the finger at teachers for low achievement.

# PRICE YOU PAY

If you don't attend school motivated to learn, constantly disrupt the lesson, show disrespect to the teacher and your peers and never suffer consequences, you will not learn, plain and simple. If you come prepared to work, learn and share, you'll learn.

At school our teachers did not allow us to fail. We had great teachers who knew that their job was to prepare us for the future. But today, when so many of our children lack family and community supports - when children in the United States need a nurturing school environment, the attention of caring and talented teachers who know their students can learn, and a rigorous curriculum that gives all students the skills to succeed in college and the work place.

The Solutions:

Inform and teach Black parents, Black families and concerned Black community members about the importance of effectively participating in the education of Black children.

Ensure that Black children are prepared socially, emotionally and academically between preschool and third grade with the basic skills they must have for educational success in higher grades. Instill strong educational values in young Black children and young Black men by making education the highest priority in the Black community.

# REDEEM YOURSELF

Establish new standards in schools and communities and new teacher expectations that promote the success of young Black men to solidify their future contributions in mainstream American society.

Give incentives that help create and maintain nurturing, effective, supportive, child – centered, two – parent families as a model for future relationships. Identify and engage strong, positive role models for young Black children and men by developing strong mentoring systems to instill positive values in Black males. Instill a strong work ethic in Black males augmented with high quality technological and literacy skills.

Many schools, teachers, administrators, superintendents, parents and elected officials want to produce successful out comes for Black males in American schools. Develop viable community vehicles, spiritual principles, positive values and developmental activities to ensure the positive social/emotional development of young Black men.

Establish a national, non - governmental, comprehensive response that is government and privately funded to manage the resources, programs, policies, ideas, advocacy and people who must solve the problem.

Our nation's public schools are failing our children.

# PRICE YOU PAY

Without a high school diploma, young Black men in America are obsolete. High expectations that result in high quality performance are often lacking. "Prayer needs to be in the schools, preserve traditional values in curriculum and protect children from radical social agendas." Help our education system.

Instead of providing a way out of poverty and discrimination, U.S. schools too often serve to perpetuate the economic and racial inequality that so poisons U.S. society, with tragic results for children and a great cost to our nation.

Many Black children and students are socially and emotionally out of control and are choosing violence and aggression as a way to solve problems in the world in which they live. They swear, fight, vandalize, challenge authority and exhibit other overly aggressive behaviors.

Black men, pull up your pants. Why are young males so violent, misdirected and unfocussed? Why are their mentalities placing them directly on the course, on becoming victims of violence, prison or the grave? "Too many of our children have little respect for authority and no fear of consequences for their actions."

Violence among Black children does not lie predominantly within schools, police or prison. This problem cannot be solved by government or social services alone.

# REDEEM YOURSELF

This war that our children are fighting against each other in the schools they attend, and against the communities in which they live, started for them in their homes.

Children have to be taught right from wrong. They need to be taught restraint and that violence is not an appropriated response to every situation. It can only be stopped in their homes; while educators, society, and government all have a role, it must be acknowledged that the parents, families, and communities of these youths hold the key to stopping violence in our schools and communities.

As a child growing up, I always felt like an outsider. I had friends but could never really feel a part of a group. I felt like something was different about me. Being a teenager with an attitude, my life took a downward spiral path of destruction. Therefore I can identify with the youth of today, and share my experience.

Character will reflect your personality or pattern of behavior. Being of good character is important, good character will take you far in life. Having an attitude caused me to be full of rage and angry at the world. My attitude causes me to be disobedient and rebellious toward authority.

I'm quoting Mr. Bill Cosby's "can't blame White people." He was criticized for drawing attention to problems in the urban community.

# PRICE YOU PAY

Cosby's language was consciously harsh, but it needed to be said. Dealing with morality and bad behavior is ripping apart Black community.

They're standing on the corner and they can't speak English. I can't even talk the way these people talk. "Why you aren't, where you is, what he drive, where he stay, where he work, who you be." And I blame the kid until I heard the mother talk, and then I heard the father talk. Everybody knows it's important to speak English... except these knuckleheads. Much mouth is what they speak!

You can't be a doctor with that kind of crap coming out your mouth. In fact you will never get any kind of job making a decent living. People march and were hit in the face with rocks to get an education, and now we've got these knuckleheads throwing that all away.

These people are not parenting. They are buying things for kids that cost five hundred dollars, but they won't spend two hundred dollars for Hook on Phonics. I am talking about these people who cry, when their son is standing there in an orange suit. Where were you when he was 18? And how come you didn't know that he had a pistol? And where is the father? Or who is his father?

People putting their clothes on backward; isn't that a sign of something gone wrong? People with their hats on backward, pants down around the crack, isn't that a sign of something?

# REDEEM YOURSELF

They're walking around with their nasty underwear showing, and holding onto their pants to keep them from falling to the ground! Or are you waiting for Jesus to pull his pants up? Isn't it a sign of something?

Why does she have her dress all the way up to her panty line, and got all types of needle piercings going through her body. What part of Africa did this come from? We are not Africans. Those people are not Africans; they don't know a thing about Africa.

Brown or Black versus the Board of Education is no longer the White person's problem. We have got to take the neighborhood back. People used to be ashamed. Today a woman has eight children with eight different "husbands" or men or whatever you call them now.

We have millionaire football players who cannot read. We have million - dollar basketball players who can't write two paragraphs. We as Black folks have to do a better job. Someone working at Wal - Mart with seven kids saying... you are hurting us.

We have to start holding each other to a higher standard. We cannot blame the White people any longer. It is not for media or anyone at this time to say whether I'm right or wrong. It is time, ladies and gentlemen, to look at the numbers. Fifty percent of our children are dropping out of high school. Sixty percent of the incarcerated males happen to be illiterate.

# PRICE YOU PAY

If Black children cannot read today, they cannot become the black doctors, nurses, lawyers, engineers, bankers, accountant, technologists, because people or educators of tomorrow who will make Black communities successful.

Why should African Americans care about achievement gaps and the quality of education in their schools? The educational achievement gap is precursor to a generational course of failure, cultural destruction and genocide.

"Those who control the education of the children, control the future of that race."

Phillip Jackson: Founder of Black Star Project

This is being referred to as the "Paper Plantation." It is better for students to drop out and get into a G.E.D. program so they may seek other forms of education, later in life, if they desire to do so.

About one third of America's youth and more than half of minority youth drop out of high school before graduation. Many of these young people have few skills that could provide them employment.

Teens having an education are very important, in order to be productive and grow with the company. It is important to know technology and to be able to operate computers. Also, it's important to be able to read.

# REDEEM YOURSELF

A lot of kids are still caught up in that I'm a gangster like mentality or I'm going to be a rapper. They are too busy worrying about chasing girls than reading books and studying for tests. They are getting suspended frequently for trying to be the class clown or school gangster.

Technology in the twenty first century is damaging. Children are hooked on electronic media, video games, and text messaging, using calculators to solve math problems. Children should be utilizing their brains, to make logical decisions.

Teens today take education for granted. They need to properly understand the importance and benefits of it. If you see someone doing something they shouldn't that doesn't mean that you should do it, too. No one should encourage you to cut or not go to school at all. This doesn't hurt anyone but you. You are the one who will feel it in the long run.

Without the ability to read well, no future exists for Black children in America. The real tragedy is that Black American students are no longer just competing against White American students. They are competing educationally against the best and the brightest students globally. And Black students are failing miserably.

# PRICE YOU PAY

Only 12 percent of African Americans in the fourth grade are proficient in reading, compared with 38 percent of Caucasian youth, and only 12 percent of African American eight graders are proficient in math, compared with 44 percent of Caucasian youth. The report shows that African youth on average fall behind from their earliest years.

Black children are at the bottom of the educational system in the United States. And because they are at the bottom of the educational system, to many of our children will end up without marketable skills, unemployed, on government assistance, in jail or dead. Many will never have decent jobs or decent lives because they did not get a good education. In addition, the proclivity to commit crimes is higher among high school dropouts than other sections of society.

If Black children cannot read today, they are really no better off than their forefathers who were slaves. Slaves' learning to read was the key to freedom. Slaves were forbidden to learn how to read, if caught reading it meant server punishment. Slaves would work in the field picking cotton, tobacco and other choirs around the plantation. They work from sun up until sun down. Late at night they'd find a secret place to learn how to read.

"It hurts inside knowing our ancestors sacrificed enormous losses and abuse to achieve privileges these children take for granted." Freedom is a beautiful thing we all take for granted.

# REDEEM YOURSELF

"There is no stronger weapon against inequality and no better path to opportunity than an education that can unlock a child's God given potential."

President Barack Obama

Individuals with at least a high school diploma earn more, work more, and are less vulnerable to layoffs. In fact, during the current recession, those with less than high school education lost jobs at nearly twice the rate of high school graduates and more than ten times the rate of college graduates.

Decades ago, it was possible for those with less than a high school education to find relatively secure jobs. But as the American economy has shifted from manufacturing of goods to service related industries, such jobs have all but disappeared.

To have any hope of success in today's labor market, individuals must demonstrate an ability to read and perform math operations at a reasonably high level. Those who cannot are unlikely ever to enjoy security, much less a middle class standard of living.

Youth will not graduate high school for various reasons, such as peer pressure or joining a gang(s), and young girls having babies. Youth are going to jail or prison at a rapid pace. School curriculum does not interest the youth, so teens believe school is a waste of time and believe they can succeed without an education.

# PRICE YOU PAY

Education:

Only forty five percent of Black men graduate from high school in the United States. Just twenty two percent of Black males who began at a four year college graduated within six years.

Sixty nine percent of Black children in America cannot read at grade level in the 4th grade, compared with twenty nine percent among White children. Seven percent of Black 8th graders perform math at grade level.

Thirty two percent of all suspended students are Black. Black students (Mostly Black males) are twice as likely as Whites to be suspended or expelled. Sixty seven percent of Black children are born out of wedlock.

When rigid rules and zero – tolerance policies are enacted, Africa American youth - particularly males are far more likely to end up in the principal's office, suspended or expelled for infractions that get other students far lesser punishment.

Black males are clearly being punished far more harshly than their peers. The suspension rate for Black males is up to five times higher than that for other student groups. Black males make up over sixty percent of all students expelled from school, even though they're only one-fourth of the student population.

# REDEEM YOURSELF

The students, who often start off with a disadvantage because of poverty, unstable backgrounds or other issues, get a double whammy when teachers and administrators make them feel unwelcome - the one place where, theoretically, everyone has an equal chance to get ahead. Even minor infractions that usually are handled with just a warning in the classroom often are met with humiliation or exclusion.

The lack of health and mental health care among low- income children is also an important factor in a child's educational development. A child's misbehavior may be a reflection of an unaddressed learning disability, mental or emotional disorder.

Regrettably, too few schools have the staff capable of recognizing the behavior of any disturbed or disabled child for what it is, and if they do, they are unable to provide treatment. More often, these children are seen as "disruptive," and instead of offering them counseling or psychological therapy, too many educators dispense "zero tolerance" discipline - usually in the form of suspension.

Suspension will now be limited to students who pose danger to persons or property or an extreme disruption to the education process or who have a history of past disciplinary problems that have led to suspensions or expulsion and where there is evidence that adminis - tration attempted to address the behavior through other means before resorting to suspension or expulsion.

90

# PRICE YOU PAY

New York Civil Liberties Union has contributed to a surge in suspensions. Since 2006, the city's suspension rate has jumped by forty percent, amounting to seventy two thousand students suspended last year, according to data published by the daily News.

Many educators and activists say suspensions are a stepping stone to dropping out. City schools follow a nationwide trend in which minority students are hit hardest by harsh punishments.

"What we're seeing in too many schools, and particularly schools that serve Black and Latino youth from low income families, is a very aggressive police presence and very heavy - handed suspension practices." Once young people are in the system, they continue the cycle of getting punished or really pushed to the prison system or to drop out and do low - wage jobs.

Many middle and high schools have full time police officers who can independently arrest children on school grounds for any number of infractions like disorderly conduct, malicious mischief and fighting that just a few years ago, such infractions would have been handle by families, the schools, or community. And now, children, as young as five and six are being hauled down to police stations in handcuffs.

# REDEEM YOURSELF

All too often, our young people do not get the education that they have a right to. They are trained to be mediocrity leads to low - paying jobs, illiteracy and crime. And each day, more and more people from our communities are facing difficulty finding decent housing, and those who have homes are struggling to just hold on to them.

Despite numerous demonstrations during the Civil Rights era for equal educational opportunities and the integration of United States schools after Brown verses Board of Education (1954), the plight of the children include attending the same schools as their White counterparts, inequities, funds to inner - city schools being misallocated, culturally insensitive teachers, and an over representation of minorities - particularly Black male - in Special Education programs.

With a little motivation and determination youths can achieve great things. All we need is a helping hand, someone to reach out and say, "I am here for you, not because I have to be but because I want to be." Young people can make valuable contributions as teens and because of this, they will have greater success as adults.

A good education in America is a major determinant of what kind of life a child will have when he or she grows up. A bad education is often a sentence to social and economic death. Education determines future income and social status as well as a child's options and quality of life.

# PRICE YOU PAY

Regardless of your age, if you dropped out of high school at some point in the past, it is likely that you have always sensed that lack of something very important. You will feel a distinct sense of accomplishment when you are able to say that you have taken this step.

Acquiring a G.E.D. makes you eligible for higher education: it will increase your chance of being accepted into college, if you are considering a career that requires further education, earning a G.E.D. is essential.

Whether you are thinking in terms of better employment, continuing education, or personal achievement, a G.E.D. is an essential step in the process. Whether you dropped out of high school quite recently, or are looking back at decades in the past, you can give yourself the chance you deserve. Your life and future can be brighter and more fulfilling.

People without a high school diploma, go back to school and receive an education. You may decide to study the G.E.D. course. Attending school could be your best choice. Studying to pass the G.E.D. course is more difficult today; the passing score has increased.

You may decide to attend college and that is possible without a high school diploma. Study and receive an associate degree, you may qualify for extra credit due to life experience.

# REDEEM YOURSELF

Colleges are offering such a program, to people who have not graduated high school.  Just imagine in less than two years, you could acquire an education.

Receiving an education is a great accomplishment. It gives you a feeling of being accepted in society. You have a high self – esteem, obtaining an education and being able to compete in the job market.

Acquiring an education did not seem important, because school appear boring and not very exciting. Education is for square people, who were not hip. Who needs to learn about history? Teachers did not teach Black History. Today I have a different perspective in regards to Education.

# TRIALS

African American youth are unaware of their culture and contributions made to the world. Children should be taught that they are part of a rich heritage of greatness; this will build their self - esteem and give them a sense of acceptance. Youth who do not know their history have no knowledge of self.

In this society, it is extremely difficult to learn about one's own people and their story through public schools and other institutions of learning. Society does not want to give recognition to the African American for their contributions to this country and the world at large.

The problem young African - Americans have in this society is that they lack knowledge of self.

# REDEEM YOURSELF

You come from a line of Kings. Many African American children grow up without any understanding that their race has made major contributions to the world.

Teaching children that they are part of a rich heritage of greatness counteracts the negativity they see and learn about their race and consequently themselves. Youth who have a greater awareness of their history, have a better sense of them self, and don't look for validation and acceptance in other places. Many will possess a higher self esteem and reach for their dreams in life.

## What is Success?

Success is doing the best you can, in as many ways as you can, it is being just and honest and true - not in a few things, but in everything you do. Always look ahead and never look back, believe you can make your dreams come true. Always believe in the best you can be and have faith in the things that you do.

Forget about mistakes you made yesterday, the lessons you learn will prove valuable for today. Never give up and think that you're through, for there is always tomorrow and a chance to begin brand new.

It is in dreaming the greatest dreams, and seeking the highest goals, that we build the brightest tomorrows. There is no limit to the goals you can attain, or the success you can achieve, your possibilities are as endless as your dreams.

# TRIALS

Whatever it is that you seek in life, whatever your dreams and what you hope to achieve, whatever you try to reach - whatever you plan...can all be yours - if you only believe you can!

Author: Larry S. Chengges

I applied to the Board of Education for a custodian position, and it required a high school diploma. It's a good feeling to pass certain requirements, such as having a high school diploma, work experience, and a back ground check.

Through good times and bad, more than one million working - age New Yorkers without a high school diploma or equivalent - nearly a quarter of the city's working - age population - find themselves on the fringes of the labor market, stuck in low wage jobs without little chance of advancement or out of work. The single biggest reason is their lack of basic skills.

Decades ago, it was possible for those with less than a high school education to find relatively secure jobs. But as the American economy has shifted from manufacturing of goods to service - related industries, such jobs have all but disappeared.

To have hope of success in today's labor market, individuals must demonstrate an ability to read and perform math operations at a reasonably high level. Those who cannot are unlikely ever to enjoy security, much less a middle class standard of living.

97

# REDEEM YOURSELF

It is no secret that the unemployment rate is staggering especially for Black men. With more and more people looking for work these days, you cannot afford to be left behind in the market place.

In order to find a decent paying job and remain gainfully employed you've got to be employable and know what kinds of work situations you best thrive in. Even more, you've got to transfer your strengths into marketable skills and attributes that add value to the work force.

The Census Bureau released information that showed the higher an American's education, the more money he or she will make on a job over his or her life time. They estimate that the difference is 3.2 million dollars in a life time.

They further state that graduating from college and getting a graduate degree amount to about 4.4 million dollars for doctors, lawyers, and other professions. This is an amount calculated over a life time of work. The normal life time of work is estimated between 25 - 64 years of age.

Money and pay scale of best jobs in America!

Anesthesiologist, $ 290.000
General Surgeon, $ 260.000
Primary Care Physician, $ 174.000
Nurse Anesthetist, $ 156.000

Product Management Director, $ 148.000
Software Engineering Director, $ 144.000
Sales Director, $ 142.000
Dentist, $ 142.000
Actuary, $ 133.000
Senior Sales Executive, $ 127.000
Software Architect, $ 110.000
Attorney, $ 118.000
Management Consultant, $ 117.000
Research and Development Manager, $ 116.000
Computer and Information Scientist, $ 115.000
Accounting Director, $ 112.000
Optometrist, $ 108.000
Emergency room Physician, $ 250.000
Obstetrician, $ 210.000
Psychiatrist, $ 185.000

A good education is a major factor of what kind of life a child will have when he or she grows up. A bad education is often a sentence to social and economic death. Education determines future income and social status as well as a child's range of future options and quality of life.

Remember When Sex Use To Be Fun?

Teen's pregnancy is at an all time high. Seventy percent of pregnant teenagers happen to be African American. What experience do teenagers have raising children, or given children proper guidance? Becoming pregnant when you're a teenager makes it difficult to graduate.

# REDEEM YOURSELF

Raising children can be indeed difficult; because you are not experience, and you are not a mature adult. Children will forever change your life; you no longer can do as you like.

You wake up in the middle of the night, because your child is having a bad dream or you have to take the child to the emergency room. During certain times of the day, you need to feed children and change the baby's pamper.

Are you going through your pregnancy alone? You tell your boyfriend you are pregnant. How did he take the news, or did he deny the baby? Will he stand by your side and attend the doctor's appointment? Would he give the child his name, and take responsibility, or claim he is not the father?

Teenage mothers are more likely to drop out of school, be financially dependent on family members, be government dependent, and suffer low - wage jobs. Additionally, their children do less well in school and are more likely to live in poverty. Black mothers have a higher infant mortality rate.

To talk about abstinence is not a bad thing, but teen girls - and boys too - need to be informed about how to protect yourself if you do have sex. Condoms, for both males and females are free in most if not all states.

# TRIALS

Black men pull your pants up. Black sisters you don't have to show a young man that you will get pregnant, so he will stay with you. There are so many young females out here with kids that have brothers and sisters by the same young man.

Condoms are given out at high schools, health fairs, hospitals, Planned Parenthood clinics, and are available at drug stores and corner stores. Protection from unwanted pregnancies and diseases is yours for the taking, yet babies are born out of wed lock every day.

"Sex is Fun until…"

*Sex is fun until you miss your period, and you start to wonder if you might be pregnant and all that this will mean for your life.
*Sex is fun until you have to tell the male or males that you had sex with that he is (or might be) the father of your unborn child.
*Sex is fun until you have to change your whole life to accommodate the new life growing within you.
*Sex is fun until your family and friends tell you that you have disappointed them and let them down.
*Sex is fun until you immediately start to feel the weight of the world come onto you.
*Sex is fun until you are at the hospital having your baby without the father because he is either at work, playing basketball, "kicking in it with his boys" or might even be having sex with another girl.

# REDEEM YOURSELF

*Sex is fun until you don't have money to buy food, milk or pampers for your baby and the father won't or can't help you with these expenses, or your mother may already be overburdened by the rest of your family who depend on her for survival.

*Sex is fun until you can't go out with your friends because you don't have anyone to watch your baby.

*Sex is fun until you will find that boys and men look at you for quick sex, not love or a relationship, because they know you have already had sex without requirements or consequences.

*Sex is fun until you will raise your child by yourself. You are the mother, father, and everything else to your child, whether you are qualified or not, whether you want to be or not.

*Sex is fun until you might become homeless because of your circumstance.

*Sex is fun until you find that you have contracted a venereal disease from having unprotected sex. You pray that it is not HIV.

*Sex is fun until you feel alone. You are alone. You are over whelmed by your circumstances and what you have allowed to happen to you.

You don't have a support system. And it seems as though you can't take the pressure of managing your life and your baby's life. "For some young girls it's an awakening where you have sex for the first time, or fall in love for the first time."

102

# TRIALS

It's an awakening when you're hanging out with your friends, and you don't know what is going to happen, but you're ready for whatever because you're young, and full of so much energy, and you have no idea that this will change your life forever. It's a night when you grow up in away, or you learn something about yourself.

This problem of inner - city violence is not New York's alone. It is every inner city across this country. From Newark, to L.A., Las Vegas to Chicago, it is not just an inner city problem; it is not just our problem. It is a national problem. And we need the nation to address it.

New York gangs are active in the schools and present a problem in neighborhoods. Gangs are more of a problem for children than crime statistics might indicate. Enormous talent, intelligence, and positive energy are being wasted as these young people are left behind. This is damaging to our communities and to the competitive strength of our country. Young people there are more positive things to do.

This war that our children are fighting against each other in the schools they attend, and against the communities in which they live, started for them in their homes. It can only be stopped in their homes.

# REDEEM YOURSELF

While educators, society and government all have a role, it must be acknowledged that the parents, families and communities of these youths hold the key to stopping violence in our schools and communities. Your criminality peaks in the hours after school when many kids are unsupervised, and tails off later in the evening when parents are home.

With parents spending less time supervising their children - some out of choice, others out of necessity for the sake of managing expenses, and a few out of sheer indifference or neglect an increasing number of youngsters are unsupervised during - out - of - school hours.

Children with uncaring parents are literally thrown to the wolves; children with all types of abusive marks - sexual abuse, incest, physical abuse, etc. are literally thrown to the wolves. And as a result of their confusion of circumstances and conditions, they had no behavioral skills and assumed that their lives were the way for most Black youths.

Sometimes, the motivation is to secure their place in a gang, providing a sense of membership that offers them misguided self - esteem. Sometimes, it comes from a tragically misguided sense of power or being caught up in drugs. Sometimes, it comes from a sense of despair and hopelessness bred by a broken home.

# TRIALS

Left ignored, what begins as rowdy, but harmless behavior can turn deadly serious. Some risky steps available to kids - joining a gang, dropping out of school, dabbling in narcotic use, getting a gun or getting arrested - can have grave, irreversible consequences.

African Americans are involved in crime, substance abuse, suicides, incarceration, feelings of hopelessness and worthlessness, poverty, poor health and unrealized potential in academic and occupational pursuits. Until we address these crimes in the Black community, youth will continue to die and not live up to their dreams.

Many Black children and students are socially and emotionally out of control and are choosing violence and aggression as a way to solve problems in the world in which they live. They swear, fight, vandalize, challenge authority and exhibit other overly aggressive behaviors. Too many of these children have little respect for authority and no fear of consequences for their actions.

Often children grow up idolizing someone with a reputation for crazy violence. It takes a strong person to say no to the pressure. Anyone dropping out of school has much time on his or her hands and is easy prey.

Many youth in inner cities have possession of guns. It appears that anyone can buy a gun, if he or she has the money.

105

# REDEEM YOURSELF

Young people have guns to stop others from picking on them in school, at parties and in the streets. They believe without guns they will be considered a punk.

Youth believe that people respect you when you have a gun, but without a gun they do not feel respected, they do not feel of value, and they do not feel appreciated. They do not understand any other way that respect can be achieved. And they do not distinguish the difference between the fear that people have for them at the point of a gun and respect for them as a person without a gun.

Times have changed. And so have people. This is a world of young people who are self - destructing before our eyes. Not all of course. And we should remind ourselves of that fact. For every young person who self - destructs, there are hundreds of others ready and able to construct and take their places.

Peer pressure is a major problem in today's society. Teens are falling under the influence of bad company that leads them in the wrong direction. Gang - related violence, schools slacking off, rebellious and trouble with the law are a few side effects of hanging with the wrong people.

You need to choose your friends; you should look for someone who will better you, who have their head on straight, and knows what they want out of life.

# TRIALS

Friends that will encourage you to do the right thing and go after your dreams, also tell you when you're messing up. And they will compliment you and say a good job.

A friend stands beside you when situation are tough and will not desert you. If I happen to show up on your door step crying, would you care? If I called and ask you to pick me up because something happened, would you come? If I need a shoulder to cry on, would you give me yours? Life is not a test; you need to know who your friends are.

We must face facts; many Black and Latino neighborhoods are infected by a plague of violence. Children are afraid to travel to and from school, and senior citizens become easy prey. Almost daily citizens young and old became victims, when they were merely doing their daily activities.

Shootings by gang members have increased as guns on the streets have proliferated. Drive - by killings are a direct result of the availability of firearms. People injure people: guns kill people.

Black on Black crime is rampant and there is little outcry against those who murder daily in the cities of America. Homicide is the leading cause of death for young Black men, with the murderous wounds in most cases inflicted by other young Black men.

# REDEEM YOURSELF

We see this unifying thread in the disruption of black families, high dropout rates, multi - generational incarceration, domestic and sexual violence, black – on - Black crime, substance abuse, depression and anxiety.

Gang violence is becoming more and more of a problem in America today. Local street gangs make it dangerous for someone to walk down the street or come home from work. Innocent people are accidentally shot or often murdered. Adults have been shot sitting outside enjoying the weather, walking to do their laundry, or even sitting at home while watching television. Children are being shot while playing in the park or walking to school.

The Black community faces a serious irony. Little more than fifty years ago, black communities wanted Blacks to protect them from White men who wore "hoods' while they killed Black people and destroyed their property.

Fifty years later, black communities are asking local (mostly White) police department and State National Guard units to protect them from our sons and neighbors; mostly young Black men in "hoodies" and ski masks who are killing Black people and destroying their property.

Are young Black men doing the work of the Ku Klux Klan as the primary killers of Black people in America?

# TRIALS

Without much debate, the answer is yes! Although Black - on - Black destruction differs from the Klan's motivation, the results are arguably more horrific.

Judging strictly by the numbers, the Klan was never as efficient as young Black men are today at killing Black people. According to a study from the Tuskegee Institute, the Ku Klux Klan killed three thousand four hundred and forty six Black people in America during an 86 - year span compared with Black men who kill about this same number of Black people every six months.

Whether perpetrated by the Ku Klux Klan or by young, black communities are being destroyed. Opportunities for positive community development and growth are smothered when young Black men murder other young Black men inadvertently main and kill other innocent people in the communities.

According to the Bureau of Alcohol, Tobacco and Firearms, there are an estimated two hundred and twenty three million firearms in the United States alone. This translates into the fact that one out of every four households owns a handgun. Guns are finding their way into hands of children and youth, as has been seen in the rash of school shootings in the last several years. The need to regulating gun sales is clear both domestically and internationally.

# REDEEM YOURSELF

Many young African American men feel angry and are desperate because Black communities and America have failed them. While some of this hopelessness is understandable because of their extreme negative circumstances, it does not give any young Black man the right to hurt others.

Gang banging, murder, prostitution, bullying, knives, and guns are just a few of the many harsh realities young people face in these resource - starved urban communities around the United States. Though this is the reality for many, there is a generation of youth who have preferred to contribute to the violence plaguing urban America.

Some statistics from the Children's Defense Fund: The three thousand and forty two deaths of children and teens from gun fire in 2007 nearly equaled the total number of U.S. combat deaths in Iraq through May 2010 (3,475). Since 1979, gun violence has ended the lives of (110,645) children and teens in America.

"They join a gang because the hierarchy makes you feel important. How do you convince a kid to stay in school when everything around him is poverty, violence, police and racism?" Youths live in communities where alcoholism, drug abuse, depression, eating disorders, pregnancies, date rape and suicides are common occurrences, but these things are not discussed until an incident occurs.

# TRIALS

There is a bigger threat in many neighborhoods, your kid has to make one of two choices; join one of the gangs, or become a victim of one. Joining a gang doesn't make you safe; it gets worst after you join. Then there are the gang wars that your kids will be fighting in. These are the kind of things that involve local street gangs, and they think they are being cool. Getting shot at is not cool at all. And with gangs comes drugs, too.

Authorities throughout the country report that gangs are responsible for most of the serious violent crimes in the major cities of the United States. Gangs engage in an array of criminal activities including assault, burglary, drive - by shootings, extortion, homicide, identification fraud, money laundering, prostitution operations, robbery, sale of stolen property, and weapons trafficking.

There are approximately thirty thousand gangs, with eight hundred thousand members, impacting twenty five hundred communities across the United States. Gangs conduct criminal activity in all 50 states and U.S. territories. Although most gang activity is concentrated in major urban areas, gangs also are proliferating in rural and suburban areas of the country as gang members flee increasing law enforcement pressure in urban areas or seek more lucrative drug markets.

Gang activity gradually increases in the 20th century. Through the 1950s and 60s, most gangs were in large cities, near towns and suburbs.

# REDEEM YOURSELF

Gangs with European ethnicity had all but disappeared, and gangs became almost exclusively Black or Latino in their membership.

While gang violence has escalated and gang involvement in drugs has been a feature of gang life for many years, gangs are increasingly and almost exclusively blamed for the drug and violence problems of the past decade. Gangs and the media both benefit from exaggerated portrayals of gangs and gang life. The best possible explanation of the relationship between gangs and violence is that it depends primarily on the gang's organization.

In the 1970s and 80s drugs became more prevalent on the street. Firearms also became easier to buy illegally. This combination made joining a street gang both more lucrative and more violent. Over all gang activity peaked in the mid 1990s.

Stanley Tookie Williams was the co – founder of the L.A. Crips. In 1981 he was convicted of murdering four people and sentenced to death at San Quentin State Prison. He was executed on December 13, 2005.

He became a famous activist fighting against the death penalty and trying to overcome gang violence, he fought up to his death. He drafted the Tookie Protocol for peace, a national street peace initiative, a frame work for peace between gangs. This legacy was founded to abolishing the death penalty.

# TRIALS

As a child, Williams heard the older kids who served time tell stories that made prison sound glamorous and fun, a place to hang out with your friends and prove how tough you were. Williams knew that prison "is no place you'd ever want to be." In his book "Life in Prison" he explains why: the cramped quarters, lack of freedom and privacy, home sickness, violence and daily indignities (strip search and having to use the toilet in public).

Some of the most notorious gangs in the United States are the Crips and Bloods. The Crips began in Los Angeles in the late 60s, partially in response to the activities of other gangs in their East L.A. neighborhood. As the gang grew in power, smaller gangs joined them until Crips affiliated gangs dominated the city.

The Bloods formed in response as the smaller non - crips sought their own power base. The Crips - Blood rivalry is vicious and never - ending, but internal strife between different: sets "within each gang" has probably resulted in more murders that the feud itself.

Today, both gangs have "franchise" gangs operating out of cities across the country. Located throughout the country, street gangs vary in size, composition, and structure. Large, nationally affiliated street gangs pose the greatest threat because they smuggle, produce, transport, and distribute large quantities of illicit drugs throughout the country and are extremely violent.

# REDEEM YOURSELF

Most gangs are loosely knit, with several members who fill leadership roles, depending on age and situation. Membership fluctuates and gang members have varying degrees of commitment to the gang. Gang cohesiveness is highest when the gang is challenged by other groups or by outsiders.

Gangs intentionally recruit children and use them to carry weapons and drugs or commit other crimes, because they tend to attract less attention from police. If caught they serve shorter sentence in juvenile detention centers than an adult gang member would serve in prison.

When a new member joins a gang, he must usually go through an initiation, initiation doesn't usually involve elaborate ceremonies or formalities, but the initiate will have to endure certain rites. The most common is "jumping in" a beating issued by all the gang members.

Gangs that accept female's gang members sometimes rape them as their initiation instead of a "jumping in," or sometimes following it, the new gang member must participate in a mission. This can be anything from stealing a car, to engaging in fighting with a rival gang. Some gangs don't consider anyone a full member until that person has shot or killed someone.

There is no easy way to stop gangs and it comes down to one thing; give people something to live for other than a gang.

# TRIALS

This can include helping at - risk youth or current gang members' help find jobs or obtain an education. Community centers bring the majority of people together to maintain their streets and show pride in where they live. Community should provide opportunities to dance, play sports, and attend games.

To have a sense of personal worth one must have a sense of self – value as a human being and have the dignity that is inherent in one's being. Having a dignity of being is having respect from others; others will then modify their behavior toward the respected person. Self respect is derived from others' perceptions and from one's own sense of efficacy.

Provide positive mentors and role models for youth, especially young Black males. Children become what they see. They are going to adopt a model of behavior and a value system that is available. If we don't have positive role models and a constructive value system for them, they will adopt negative models and the destructive system.

In fact, negative role models and a destructive value system are heavily market to our children. Without a counter marketing strategy, we have little chance of reaching, impressing and persuading our children not to be violent.

We must provide an education that proposes our youth to become a viable part of our society.

# REDEEM YOURSELF

They must have economic alternatives and practical reasons not to engage in negative, destructive behaviors. We have not helped most young men to obtain the necessary skills to be successful in life.

When I was a child, I spoke as a child; I understood as a child, I thought as a child, but when I became a man, I put away childish things.

Corinthians 13:11

September 7, 2007 the Daily News Paper reads (Warning may be killing kids). Rates of Teen suicide sky rocketed after the Food and Drug Administration required strict "black box" warnings on antidepressants for children.

Doctors are claiming that children are having various mental conditions and they believe that children must be treated. Want to prescribe psychotropic medicine, because children have a behavior problem, or because they are hyper. Doctors believe that giving children medicine is the answer.

Doctors may be more likely to prescribe drugs to Medicaid patients, because the public insurer pays significantly less for non - drug treatment, such as counseling than private insurance companies. It may also be harder for poorer families to make it to regular therapy appointments.

# TRIALS

Children on Medicaid were significantly more likely to be prescribed antipsychotic drugs for "conduct disorders" such as hyperactivity, aggression or defiance than middle class children, who were more likely to be prescribing the drugs for severe mental conditions.

Poor children are vastly more likely to be given antipsychotic drugs than middle class children, and often for less serious conditions. Children between the ages 6 - 17 were being prescribe antipsychotics; less than 1 percent of children with private insurance were given the drugs.

Antipsychotics are approved only for conditions such as schizophrenia, bipolar disorder and autism, but the law allows doctors to prescribe as they see fit. The drugs have a sedating effect; they are becoming more and more popular as treatments for attention deficit disorder, even though no studies have been done on their effectiveness for that use.

Youth prescriptions for the drugs fell 22 percent in 2004, after the medications were labeled as increasing the risk of suicide among kids who took them. That year, teen suicides rose by 14 percent among 5 - 19 year olds, according to a study in September's American Journal of Psychiatry. The suicide rate rose by 8 percent in 2003 - 04 for people ages 10 - 24, the Centers for Disease Control and Prevention reported yesterday that it scored 76 percent for teen girls.

# REDEEM YOURSELF

African Americans are more often misdiagnosed with schizophrenia and mood disorders than Caucasian people. However, despite these troubling issues, it is increasingly vital that African Americans seek approate services. For instance, suicide rate increased among African Americans ages 10 – 14 across a recent fifteen year span.

"Mental disorders and mental health problems appear in families of all social classes and of all backgrounds. No one is immune! Yet there are children who are at greater risk, by virtue of a broad array of factors. These include physical problems: intellectual disabilities, retardation; family history of mental and addictive disorders, poverty, and caregiver separation or abuse and neglect."

Emotional, behavior, and mental disorders cut across all income, education, racial, and religious groups. Children who have these disorders live with single parents and two parent families, adoptive, and foster families. They live in every community across the country and attend every school.

California is a common place to treat children diagnosed with attention deficit hyperactivity disorder, or ADHD, with marijuana. California voters passed a law allowing doctors to recommend medical marijuana to their patients, including those under the age of eighteen.

# TRIALS

I disagree with California's law on giving marijuana to children, because of the serious effects. It causes children to become dysfunctional, also unable to be productive in society. People, including me, would say marijuana is not safe. Smoking marijuana could lead to the use of other drugs.

Children who use marijuana at a young age are also at significantly higher risk for the development of a mental disorder. Marijuana used at a young age can cause adverse effects that plague the users for the rest of their lives.

ADHD is described as a neurological disorder that prevents children from focusing on a specific task. In essence, people with ADHD have difficulty with self - regulation and self - motivation due to problems with distractibility, organization, and prioritization.

Notably, these are the same functions that are most impaired by marijuana use. Get it? Pot actually exacerbates the problems with attention, memory and concentration that you want a treatment for ADHD to alleviate.

Statistics show urgency. It is reported that there has been a rise of 22 percent in cases of Attention Deficit Hyperactivity Disorder (ADHD) since 2003. Now with the diagnosis comes a prescription of pharmaceuticals whose effect on the body is not known. We know that drugs are a big business and our children are at risk when corporate interests are calling the shots.

# REDEEM YOURSELF

How do your children behave at home, or play in school? Does their behavior leave a lot to be desired? Research has shown that food additives such as sugar, coloring and other chemicals may cause some children to exhibit poor health, poor learning and unacceptable behavior. The behavioral problems cited included an inability to concentrate and restlessness, which could contribute to difficulty with school work.

In our educational systems, when children misbehave or do poorly in their studies, they are placed in special education classes and sometimes given drugs to keep them calm and quiet. If your child has difficulty in school, you should pay more attention to what he or she is eating or drinking.

Young people miss out on valuable time in school. Many are often too troubled to learn without special help and when they don't get it, they may bounce in and out of school. When children can't learn in school and drop out or are suspended or expelled, communities face the prospect of having unproductive children and youth "hanging around" and creating concerns about safety and crime for themselves and others.

Mental difficulties often surface during childhood and when they are severe, they create enormous suffering for the children and all members of their families suffer a diminished quality of life.

# TRIALS

The lack of health and mental health care among low - income children is also an important factor in a child's educational development. A child's misbehavior may be a reflection of an unaddressed learning disability, mental or emotional disorder. Regrettably, too few schools have the staff capable of recognizing the behavior of a disturbed or disabled child, and if they do, they are unable to provide treatment.

These children are seen as "disruptive" and instead of offering them counseling or psychological therapy, too many educators dispense "zero Tolerance" discipline - usually in the form of suspensions or expulsions. These approaches have serious negative consequences. Numerous studies have demonstrated that students who are suspended or expelled are more likely than their peers to eventually drop out of school.

The consequences of children being on psychotropic medicine are very dangerous. The consequences include not being in touch with reality, causing children to face difficulties in life, such as not completing school, not getting a job, being homeless, or going to prison and etc. The possibilities are great for children committing serious crimes, or being confined to an institution.

There are those who say that serving children with emotional, behavioral, and mental health problems is too costly. Yet, the alternative is even more expensive. Consider not intervening early with children and the possibility of serious mental health problems will occur.

Families will miss work if call to school about their children's problems, or if they have to stay home to care for them. Communities lose valuable workers when there is this kind of family disruption. The staggering emotional and financial toll on families can also affect their productivity on the job.

While most people are not ashamed about seeking primary care for a physical health concern, there is still a great deal of shame associated with accessing mental health care. Working with a mental health professional does not solely need to focus on issues of mental illness.

African - American men and women may not seek therapy for fear of appearing weak or being considered crazy. Therapy and counseling can help with a variety of emotional issues, and promote positive personal growth from relationships and work - related issues - such as self - esteem and anger management.

About one in three African Americans who need care receive it. Furthermore, African Americans are also more likely than other racial ethnic group to terminate treatment. The problem is that African Americans are over represented in psychiatric hospitals and emergency rooms, which indicated that they do not seek services until a crisis has occurred, and their symptoms are more severe.

TRIALS

The one reality that people need to keep in mind, is that those who seek out therapy are relatively healthy in other areas of their lives, and can greatly benefit from psychotherapy and counseling.

Psychologist can work with clients on anxiety and depression concerns, they can also address a variety of issues from career barriers to relationship troubles to "just feeling stuck" in one's life journey.

Whether dealing with parenting issues, addressing work - related stress, clarifying career concerns or understanding how best to handle family conflict, more African Americans must believe that they can benefit from accessing culturally competent psychological services as part of their overall wellness plan.

Stress caused by racism and discrimination "places minorities at risk for mental disorders such as depression and anxiety. Stress and angst associated with dealing with racism and discrimination are directly linked to the poor physical and mental health of many minorities.

## WE SHALL SURVIVE

During the past few decades, the United States prison system has fallen into a cruel era of social vengeance, unlike any other in our nation's history. While crime rates rose and fell, our rate of incarceration sky rocketed at unprecedented rates. We now imprison our citizens at 6 - 10 times the rate of most other industrialized countries. In fact, we have the world's highest rate of imprisonment.

Prison population has exploded from three hundred thousand to more than two million people in a few decades, because of rampant crime. The truth however does not explain the sudden and dramatic mass incarceration of African Americans. This is because the country's incarceration rate has roughly quintupled since the early 1970s.

# REDEEM YOURSELF

More than two million Americans currently live behind bars in jails, state prisons, federal penitentiaries: many millions more are on parole or probation.

Currently, there are more than (2, 300.000) people incarcerated in the United States prison system. The tough - on - crime policies of the 1980s and 90s that included trying juveniles as adults, eliminating parole, the privatization of building prisons, the expansion of mandatory minimum sentencing, three strike laws and incarcerating low level drug offenders rather than providing drug abuse treatment, have all led to an ever increasing prison population.

There are more Black men in prisons and jails in the United States (about 1.1 million) than there are Black men incarcerated in the rest of the world combined. "We have the highest rate of incarceration of any place in the world." This criminalization process now starts in elementary schools with black male children as young as six and seven years old being arrested in staggering numbers according to a 2005 report, education on Lock down by the Advance Project.

And the vast majority of that increase is due to the war on drugs. Drug offenses alone account for about two thirds of the increase in the federal inmate population, and more than half of the increase in the state prison population.

# WE SHALL SURVIVE

Since 1980, the number of women in prison has increased at nearly double the rate of men. There are now nearly seven times as many women in state and federal prisons as there were in 1980 (12,300). By mid - 2000, there were about (156,200) female inmates in state and federal prisons and local jails, representing about 7 percent of the local prison population.

Women represent the fastest growing segment of prison and jail population. Five percent of incarcerated women serve time for nonviolent crimes. In 1970, there were five thousand and six hundred women incarce - rated in federal and state prisons. At year end 2000, ninety one thousand and six hundred twelve women were in state or federal prisons 6.6 percent of the total prison population.

Women prisoners are often survivors of abuse, and once incarcerated, routinely experience sexual harassment. Forty four percent of women under correctional authority, including 57 percent of the women in state prisons, report that they were physically or sexually abused at some point in their lives. Sixty nine percent of women report that this abuse occurred before age 18. Many women in prisons and jails in the United States are victims of sexual abuse by staff, including male guards touching prisoner's breasts and genitals when conducting searches.

Fact sheet: Women in Prison

# REDEEM YOURSELF

*Since 1980 the number of women in prison has increased at nearly double the rate of men.

*The number of women in state and federal prisons has increase seven - fold from twelve thousand and three hundred in 1980 to ninety six thousand in 2002.

*Women in prison are 43 percent African Americans and 12 percent Latinos.

*In 1997, Latinos (44%) and African American women (39%) were more likely to be incarcerated for a drug offense than white women (23%).

*Three – quarters of women in state and federal prisons report that they had used drugs regularly prior to their arrest; over 60 percent had used drugs in the month prior to their offense.

*In 1997, 65 percent of women in state prisons were parents of minor children, compared to 55 percent of men. Two –thirds of mothers incarcerated in state prison lived with their children prior to their arrest.

*Approximately 37 percent of women and 28 percent of men in prison had monthly incomes of less than six hundred dollars prior to their arrest.

*nearly a quarter of women in state prisons have a history of mental illness.

*Nationally 3.6 percent of women in state and federal prison were HIV positive in 2000, compared to 2 percent of men. The women's figures range as high as 18.2 percent in New York State and 41 percent in the District of Columbia.

*More than half of the women in state prisons have been abused, 47 percent physically abused and 39 percent sexually abused 9with many being survivors of both types of abuse).

# WE SHALL SURVIVE

Politicians and criminal justice/law enforcement officials target and victimize African American and Latino youth for the sole purpose of supporting the economic structure and stability of Up State New York Counties. Youth need to know the truth about the many traps, swindles, and pitfall Politicians, criminal justice officials, and business institutions have erected and put into place for our youth.

## Youth Confined in OCFS Facilities

In 1899, the first juvenile court was established in Chicago. By 1927, 47 states followed suit. Between 1966 and 1975, Supreme Court rulings further established juveniles' due process rights. Decades of advocacy and reform efforts have produced the Juvenile Justice and Delinquency Prevention Act (JJDPA) of 1974. Reauthorized in 2002, it awaits fiscal support through the budget process.

The New York State of Children and Family Services (OCFS) is the state agency responsible for the incarceration or placement of juveniles (children under age 16 at the time of arrest). A youth confined in an OCFS placement facility may be transferred to an adult prison at age 16 at the discretion of a judge, or at 18 at the discretion of OCFS. At age 21, a youth is automatically transferred to the Department of Correctional Services (DOCS) to serve the rest of his or her time in adult prison.

# REDEEM YOURSELF

Judges frequently resort to incarceration not to protect society, but because there are no better alternatives for kids who are emotionally unstable or addicted to drugs. In fact, mental health and drug treatment in these facilities is often nonexistent.

There are over a half - million children and youth in our foster care system many of them victims of abuse, neglect or abandonment. A third of them enter the system at age 13 or older, and thousands of them will "age- out" before a permanent home is found. And for all too many, the problem of the Family Court becomes the problem of the juvenile Court becomes the problem of the judicial system.

On any given day, hundreds of youth under the age of 16 are incarcerated in the New York City Department of Juvenile Justice's three youth jails: the Horizons, Crossroads, and Bridges (aka Spot ford) juvenile detention centers. The majority of the young people locked up in these secure detention centers are charged with non - violent, low - level offenses and do not pose any threat to public safety.

New York Times – New York Merges Juvenile Justice and Child Welfare Agencies, city signals intent to put fewer teenagers in jail. The Bloomberg Administration plans to merge the city's Department of Juvenile Justice into its child welfare agency, signaling a more therapeutic approach toward delinquency that will send fewer of the city's trouble teenagers to jail.

# WE SHALL SURVIVE

City officials said that under the new arrangement, youth who commit crimes, but are not considered dangerous will have easier access to an expanding assortment of in - home programs managed by the Administration for Children's Services, the child welfare agency.

This will allow them to stay in their neighborhood with their families while following a strict set of rules requiring them to stay out of trouble, keep curfews and meet educational goals. Juvenile offenders, usually between the ages of 11 - 16 years old, are typically in the custody of the Department of Juvenile Justice before the trial and sentencing.

We need to completely revamp the juvenile justice system, the way we think about juvenile justice and the way it impacts our communities. We need to break the cradle - to prison pipe line that entraps so many of our youth, especially those of color. The future of our youth, and our nation, hangs in the balance.

The type of community base therapy, meant to set young offenders on more productive paths in life, is a growing alternative to sending youth to notorious state run juvenile prisons, which a state task force recently described as broken, ineffective and dangerous. The prisons are also expensive, costing the state and city two thousand fifteen dollars per youth annually.

# REDEEM YOURSELF

The department that handles about five thousand five hundred offenders a year, places them in group homes or in one of three detention centers. A judge's typical options at sentencing are to release offenders on probation, or send them to one of the state's juvenile prisons, or residential facilities run by nonprofit organization.

National data indicates that 75 percent of incarcerated children are from single - parent's households and 77 percent of these children are African American or Latino. Many young Black men in America are barely surviving or no longer exist. The tragedy can be seen in prisons and jails across America, where Black men make up 50 percent to 80 percent of the prison population.

Rates of imprisonment in 2001 were highest among Black males (32.2%) and Latino males (17.2%) and lowest among White males (6.9%). About 19 percent of Black men in their twenties who were not college students were either in jail or in prison.

Blacks account for only 12 percent of the population, but 44 percent of all prisoners in the United States are Black. Blacks who compromise only 12 percent of the population and account for about 13 percent of drug users, constitute 35 percent of all arrests for drug possession, 55 percent of all convictions on those charges, and 74 percent of all those sentenced to prison for possession.

# WE SHALL SURVIVE

In at least fifteen states, Black men were sent to prison on drug charges at rates ranging from twenty to fifty – seven times those of White men. In 1986, before mandatory minimums for crack offenses became effective, the average federal drug offense sentence for Blacks was 11 percent higher than for Whites.

Years later following the implementation of harsher drug sentencing laws, the average federal drug offense sentence was 49 percent higher for Blacks. Blacks are seven times more likely to go to prison or jail than Whites.

Almost 60 percent of black males are high school dropouts in their early thirties, and have spent time in prison. The percentage of young jobless Black men continues to increase, part of a trend that generally hasn't abated in decades. In 2000, about 65 percent of black males high - school dropouts had no jobs, either because they could not find work, or because they were in jail.

In several states persons as young as 16 or 17 are treated as adults in the criminal justice system, while the juvenile system provides rehabilitative programs, youth in the adult system receive little of these programs. Youth are at greater risk of assault and victimization in the adult system, and cannot expunge their criminal records, which will dramatically limit their future opportunities in employment and education.

# REDEEM YOURSELF

Jails and prisons are dangerous places for anybody, but especially for children and teens. Many of these institutions house vicious predators who have been locked up for brutal violent crimes. Yet on any given day, approximately nine thousand – five hundred juveniles under the age of 18 are locked up in adult prisons. Children, as young as 15, can be prosecuted as adults in many states without review by a judge or a court hearing.

In numerous cases, there is no public safety justification for locking up these young people in adult prisons. Juveniles may be held in adult jails for months or even years, although most of them are not charged with a violent crime and many will not be convicted of any crime. Never the less, they languish behind bars with dangerous criminals and are at great risk of being raped and beaten. Many are pushed to attempt suicide.

Once arrested, defendants are generally denied meaningful legal representation and pressured to plead guilty, whether they are or not. Once convicted virtually every aspect of one's life is regulated and monitored by the system.

It is clear that too many young Black males are unfairly defined as criminals by an unfair and discriminatory American system; many young Black males have allowed themselves to be conditioned for the new prisons being built for them. The same happened when crack cocaine wasted a generation of young Black males and females.

133

# WE SHALL SURVIVE

Many young inmates walk out more damaged and dangerous than when they arrived with three quarters of them committing new crimes within three years. Up state law makers were only too happy to welcome juvenile jails in their districts as a form of economic development – even if it meant dragging inmates hundreds of miles away from their families and friends.

The problem of low self - esteem is not generally a wide spread problem for children of the majority population; however, for the children seen in the juvenile system, low self - esteem is a significant problem that is presented and may have been pivotal in their entry into the system.

The majority of the children seen in the juvenile justice system are from dysfunctional families, not having a normal family ambiance - hence, they enter the juvenile justice system having very low self - esteem. Many have actually experienced physical abuse at the hands of police and "The System," as the bureaucracy of the juvenile/criminal legal justice system. And most who enter the system leave it worst than when they entered.

Many middle and high schools have full time police officers who independently arrest children on school grounds for any number of infractions like disorderly conduct, malicious mischief and fighting that just a few years ago, these infractions would have been handled by families, the schools or community.

# REDEEM YOURSELF

And now, children as young as five and six are being hauled down to police stations in handcuffs.

Most African American males have experienced the pain of discrimination, racial hatred, rejection, personal and emotional attacks, and the stereotypes that deny individuality any importance.

The media and social services need to provide better values in their work, be accurate and fair in their presentation by placing higher value on truth and decency, be responsible with their influence, and bring positive change to our culture.

The news media shows countless reports of black youth doing drugs, selling drugs, and engaging in gang violence. Those reports rarely probe the depths of these realities, and they're not generally balanced by reports of success and achievement. Black youth are not inherently criminal. They are not deviant and pathological. All children yearn to belong, to create, to understand the world around them.

The news media reports crime, especially violent crimes, out of proportion to its actual occurrence, violent crimes dominates crime coverage. Although homicides made up one to two - tenths of one percent of all arrests, homicides made up more than a quarter (27% - 29%) of all the crimes on the evening news.

# WE SHALL SURVIVE

African Americans are underrepresented in reporting as victims and over represented in the news as perpetrators. Articles about White homicide victims tend to be longer, and more frequent than the articles that cover African Americans victim.

African Americans were 22 percent more likely to be shown on local TV news in Los Angeles committing violent crimes than non violent crimes. Actual crime statistics reveal African Americans were equally likely to be arrested for violent crimes. Another series of studies showed that Whites committed more violent crimes than were represented by television crime stories of violent crimes.

Youth of color fare far worse than their white counter-parts in the media's association of youth and violence. A study of Time and Newsweek stories found that the term "young black males" became synonymous with the word "criminal" in coverage. A study on TV news showed that white youth were more likely to be featured in stories on health or education than black youth.

Violence against youth is under reported. Studies found that crimes by adults against youth are under reported, and the public thinks youth commit a far larger share of all crimes than they actually do.

The first solution is to combat the negative images and teachings that have been propelled upon us by school systems and the media.

# REDEEM YOURSELF

From the cradle to the prison population, children in the 4$^{th}$ grade are given test(s); the test will decide how many prisons to build in the future.

The cradle to prison pipeline is an urgent national crisis that leaves a Black child born in 2001 with a one in three risk of going to prison and a Latino child with one in six risks. The prison pipeline is fueled by pervasive poverty. Inadequate health and mental health care, gaps in early childhood development, disparate educational opportunities, chronic abuse and neglect and over burdened and ineffective juvenile justice systems.

High school dropouts are almost three times as likely to be incarcerated, as youth who have graduated from high school. But dropouts are not the only ones who encounter entry ways into the prison pipeline.

Our children drop - out, or pushed out of school, the prison pipeline is only one move away. With lack of activities and many community centers closed during the week, children head to the street corner. A different type of educational institution teaches antisocial values, like violence and criminal behavior.

Young Black men without a job and without an education become at - risk for involvement in the criminal justice system. Without work, without school, and without a diploma, young Black men are vulnerable to the prison pipeline.

137

# WE SHALL SURVIVE

When our young people get into the criminal justice system, it is a revolving door of criminality because the prisons no longer even try to reform or rehabilitate the offenders. The system is only about punishment. The services in education and training do not exist as they did in the past.

Five years in the pen can easily become ten which can easily turn into twenty which can easily lead to lifelong confinement or death row if you resort to street justice. Only you can decide how you are going to handle your situation, but at least do this: Think long and hard about the boomerang effects of your decision before you rush out and do something that could make your situation worse.

Mandatory minimums have been greatly increasing the prison population, and have contributed to racial injustices in the criminal system. One particular egregious form of mandatory minimum sentencing is the disparity between crack and powder cocaine.

And then, for the most part, the prisoners come out being better criminals than they were going in - or, even worst, they come out criminalized when they could have received alternative sentencing and assistance, which could have led them to be productive members of society.

Our children are victims of a terrible conspiracy.

# REDEEM YOURSELF

There is a conspiracy to destroy them, and we see people being marginalized, the next stage of that marginalization is their extinction. What better way to do it than bring guns into our community, drugs into our community, aids into our community and exploit our sex drive?

We have lost a generation of black children and the cycle of insanity continues in the twenty first century. We are losing children to education, employment, economics, incarceration, health, housing, and parenting.

The question that remains is will we lose the next two or three generations, or possibly every generation of black children here after to the streets, negative media, gangs, drugs, poor education, unemployment, father absence, crime, violence, and death?

Some people go through their whole lives never taking responsibility for the choices they make in life. They over step the appropriate boundary, act with hostile intent, refuse to abide by the law, inflict pain and misery on others, and then deny any wrong doing on their part when it's time to face the consequences of their actions.

Do not put yourself in situations to become an accessory to something because you did not have the common sense or will power to keep it moving. Leave no time in your schedule for anything else except the things that you are doing to build and grow.

Take classes and attend seminars to educate yourself. Join the community board and volunteer somewhere to make a difference.

How important are the right friends? We know that people get into crime and gangs primarily because their friends do. Hanging around with delinquent friends encourages young people to think of themselves as delinquents, and puts them in a world where criminal behavior is easy to engage in and brings social rewards.

"Young people have given up on society as a result of the obstacles they face, instead of fighting back; they join the subculture of drugs and crime as a means of what they believe will up lift them from poverty. So you have this inner change of what is cool and hip in the hood and what is cool and hip in prison. You have a rotating door."

Often times when you're young, you may think it's all about you and nothing else seems to matter. You may believe that the world owes you something and think you are entitled to behave in such a manner. You have this notion, you can do as you please, and believe that you're indestructible.

You have the wrong concept, it is not all about you, and you cannot do as you please. Do not believe for a second that society will allow you to run rampant and cause havoc. Society is the power that is the people rule and passes judgment against you.

# REDEEM YOURSELF

Your buddies and you are hanging out, running throughout the neighborhood all hours of the night, committing various crimes and getting high. You are behaving in a manner that is not acceptable. Whatever happens, you are a part of it, and you do not want to be considered a punk. Your manhood and foolish pride will not allow you to think different.

Tragedy has struck the crew; your partner(s) been murdered, or seriously injured. So, you're possibly on the run, because you have committed a serious crime, and an all points bulletin is out for your arrest. It is only a matter of time before you are caught.

Friend you grew up with in the neighborhood, which might've attended the same school and played certain games, cut class to hang out or go to hooky parties, and get high, also indulge in criminal activities. Being associated in gang violence and hanging on the street corners, you believe this constitutes friendship.

If you get into trouble, see how many friends offer you help. Your friend(s) and you get arrested. How quick will these friend(s) turn on you? What will they say or do to save themselves? Friends are too busy in the street; they don't have the time to visit, or write you a letter or send you money for commissary.

Everything you do in life is the result of a choice. When you are outside the walls of a prison, you have more choices than you do inside. You can decide if you are going to get out of bed or sleep in.

141

# WE SHALL SURVIVE

You are surrounded by rules and those rules are enforced.

So ask yourself "Do I need the structure that prison life forces upon me, or can I make choices that will allow me to be a man to my family?" prison will always be a hostile environment; it has to be so that the prison staff can justify the need for their jobs and the use of physical force.

Across this nation, countless young men and women, like you, are vegetating in juvenile halls and in youth authorities. More and more prisons are being constructed to accommodate your generation when you grow to adulthood.

Between the drugs, violence, lack of economic independence, and proper educational systems and resources, our kids are really paying the ultimate price. They are losing their youth, their innocence and their freedom, to a way of life that is not conducive to them realizing a positive future.

Mother! Would tell me, "Son be careful of the friends you choose." She would check out my friends upon their visit, and she'd voice her opinion. She'd say the company you keep is very important, because it is easy to get into trouble but hard to get out.

Like when you're hanging out with your friends and you don't know what's going to happen but you're ready for whatever goes down.

142

# REDEEM YOURSELF

You're young and full of energy and you have no idea that this is going to be the night, that is going to change your life forever. It is a night where you grow up in some way or you learn something about yourself.

Questions for you to consider: Is there anything that you have done in your life that you are taking full responsibility for? Who are you blaming and why? When are you going to hold yourself accountable for your choices and actions?

Do you believe remorse above accountability? Are you still playing the blame game? What does remorse mean to you? Are you remorseful for anything you've ever done in your life? If yes, what have you done to make things right? What else can you do?

Many teenagers' description of manhood defines these perceptions: what they imagine is male behavior, complete with public drinking, loud obscenities, homophobia and vulgar come – on to women.
*How much money they have
*Amount of sexual intercourse
*The propensity to be violent
*There interaction with the criminal justice system

Manhood is challenged by your ability to adhere to the responsibilities of the situations you create for yourself. That means moral responsibility is paramount to achieving a level of manhood to be admired and respected.

143

# WE SHALL SURVIVE

*Your ability and willingness to protect and provide
*Your desire to love and honor
*Your adherence to responsibilities
*Your positive and responsible interaction with the world around you

I have seen many young people including myself, with good minds; loose themselves to drugs and violence as they searched for their identity and adulthood. There were multiple reasons to use drugs, but very few reasons or rational not to use. I spent my adolescent years angry and confused.

Too many young men have turn to gangster rap, romanticized whatever notions involved in its lyrics, then started their floundering in school until they drop out and then wander in their own uncertain jungle, perfecting an ability to do nothing of any significance, while revolving through the juvenile and criminal justice system doors; a place they connect with main stream society, have conditioned themselves to accept as their station in life: a state prison cell.

Black men pull your pants up. Why so many of our young males are so violent, misdirected, and unfocused? Why are their mentalities placing them directly on the course of becoming victims of violence, prison or the grave?

# REDEEM YOURSELF

President Ronald Reagan signed the Anti – Drug Abuse Act of 1986 and 1988, this included mandatory penalties for crack cocaine offenses that were the harshest ever adopted for low - level drug offenses.

Fears about drugs in the 1980s - particularly with the newest drug at the time, crack cocaine – created a political environment that invested in a punitive approach to substance abuse by legislating long sentences for drug offenses at the federal and state levels.

This distinction has contributed to an over whelming racial disparity in the federal prison system, where 80 percent of persons serving time for crack offense are African American. It also has disproportionately incarcerated low - level crack cocaine offenders rather than drug kingpins and international drug traffickers, which the federal government says it prioritizes.

As a result of the "War on Drugs." America's incarceration policies have disproportionately impacted minorities, particularly African Americans. While African Americans constitute only 13 percent of drug users, they represent 74 percent of those sentenced to prison for drug possession. The horrifying result has been that one in three black men between the ages of 20 and 29 are under some form of criminal justice control.

# WE SHALL SURVIVE

Substance abusers who live in more affluent communities are not subject to random "war on drug" stop - and – frisks, traffic stops or area "sweeps" by local police.

More affluent substance abusers can access medical treatment for their problem using health insurance benefits. On the other hand, low – income communities, many of which are communities of color, are the usual targets of drug laws and enforcement crack downs.

For many drug users, crime and addiction are closely intertwined. Users are prosecuted for possessing, using, or distributing drugs and drug paraphernalia (including syringes). Some users commit crimes to obtain drugs or money to buy drugs. Many are under the influence of drugs when they commit crimes.

That is one reason why people of color now account for more than 60 percent of the people who are incarcerated in U.S. jails and prisons although studies consistently show that people of color are no more likely to use or sell drugs than Whites. With felony criminal records, low – income substance abusers and their families are banished to an even lower socioeconomic status.

REDEEM YOURSELF

The imprisonment of blacks for drug offenses is part of a larger of over incarceration in the United States. Although prison should be used as a last resort to protect society from violent or dangerous individuals, more people are sent to prison in the United States for nonviolent drug offenses than for crimes of violence.

Throughout the 1990s, more than one hundred thousand drug offenders were sent to prison annually. More than 1.5 million prison admissions on drug charges have occurred since 1980. The rate at which drug offenders are incarcerated has increased nine fold.

## YOU CAN BE A WINNER

Drug users who have been arrested will serve their time in various correctional settings, tried, and convicted to serve their sentences in various settings. The judge or jury chooses a setting based on the nature of the crime and the length of the sentence imposed. They also consider other factors, such as the age and gender of the individual and any prior convictions.

Jails are administered by a county or city, individuals convicted of misdemeanors, such as possessing small amounts of drugs, serve their time in jails. Jails also house people awaiting hearings, trials, or transfers to prison. Sentences are usually less than one year.

148

# REDEEM YOURSELF

State prisons house people convicted of felonies under state law, such as selling illegal drugs or committing a violent crime to support an addiction. State drug users serve their time in jail or state prison. Federal prisons house people convicted of violating federal laws, such as interstate drug trafficking.

The criminal justice system also uses other approaches. Some are alternatives to prison or jail; others are used in conjunction. The main ones: Probation allows the convicted person to remain at liberty but subjected to conditions and restrictions, such as frequent drug testing or substance abuse treatment.

Parole is the conditional release of a prisoner before his or her full sentence has been served; individuals on parole must abide by certain conditions imposed by the parole board or be returned to prison.

Drug court is an approach in which a defendant accused of a nonviolent crime is offered the opportunity to plead guilty to the charges, with the promise that if he or she complies with court – mandated substance abuse treatment, the court will dismiss the charges. Frequent drug testing is a prominent feature of the drug court approach.

Two million inmates are now in U.S. prisons and jails, nearly four times the 1980 count. More than four million persons are on parole or probation. How did we get to this circumstance?

# YOU CAN BE A WINNER

Since the 80s, the United States has waged a "war on drugs" mandatory long term sentencing has steadily increased the prison population.

The Rockefeller Drug Laws have had a devastating effect on communities of color in New York. More studies have shown that proportionally, people of all races use drugs at equal rates.

Yet although people of color comprise approximately 23 percent of New York State's population, they comprise fully 91 percent of those incarcerated for drug felonies. There are more Blacks and Latinos entering the prison system for drug offenses each year.

The overcrowding of prisons has led to corporate interest in building prisons. Prison overcrowding has led to greater violence against prisoners, who are often without access to judicial resource. As prisons become more populated, prisoners are then housed farther away from families, necessary networks and resources.

The prison industrial complex contributes to the dilemma of seeking the proper response to crime. Under this condition, there has been an increased use of super max prisons, control units of severe isolation. Impoverished rural areas are encouraged to build prisons; offenders from cities are shipped states away from families and communities. Some states can't fill prison beds, yet others are trying to scrape together finances for more prison construction.

# REDEEM YOURSELF

For the tycoons who have invested in the prison industry, it has been like finding a pot of gold. They don't have to worry about strikes or paying unemployment insurance, vacations or comp time. All of their workers are full time, and never arrive late or absent because of family problems: moreover, if they don't like the pay of 25 cents an hour and refuse to work, they are locked up in isolation cells.

The police system, the juvenile and criminal justice system and the prison system all benefit Whites more than anyone in this nation. They get more than their share of the jobs and they benefit congressionally from prison numbers in a district (usually rural) that counts the prisoners as residents of that district, but those prisoners can't vote or have any say in what goes on. And those who are not in prison but are ex – felons are also restricted from voting.

Prison is a business where the warden lives in the area, the cook, the correction officers, the man that distributes the food and other supplies from his own business, that he started when he realized there was a need, because of the prisons, they all live there and profit off of the large number of inmates in their all white town.

It seems that government is willing to pay billions of dollars to lock up young black men, rather than the millions it would take to prepare them to become viable contributors and valued members of our society.

151

"Remember, prisons are big business and their profit increases as our youth are incarcerated in the school – to – prison pipeline."

The real crime in America are being committed by greedy people who manipulate Government Legislation, law enforcement practices and criminal justice policy to make youths commodities for other people to make a living and prosper.

"United States employers have pointed to the tight labor market for their interest in employing prisoners. But the other advantages, though not stated publicly, are obvious."

The prison system provides an "ideal" workforce: employers do not have to pay health or unemployment insurance, vacation time, sick leave or overtime. They can hire fire or reassign inmates as they so desire, and can pay the workers as little as 21 cents an hour. The inmates cannot respond with a strike, file a grievance, or threaten to leave and get a better job.

In addition, during the last 20 years more than 30 states have passed laws permitting the use of convict labor by commercial enterprises. These programs now exist in 36 states. Prisoners can be forced to work for pennies because they have no rights. Even the constitution's 14th amendment which abolished slavery, excludes prisoners from its protection.

# REDEEM YOURSELF

One can buy stock in the booming businesses now and the longer they keep someone locked up, the more money they make.

Inmates are required to work if they are medically able. Institution work assignments include employment in areas like food service or the warehouse, or work as an inmate orderly, plumber, painter, or groundskeeper. Inmates earn from 8 cents to $ 1.00 per hour for work assignments.

It may surprise some people that as the number of people without jobs increases, the number of working people actually increase – they become prison laborers. Everyone inside has a job.

There are currently over 70 factories in California's 33 prisons alone. Prisoners do everything from textile work and construction, to manufacturing and service work. Prisoners make shoes, clothing, and detergent, they do dental lab work, recycling, metal production, and wood production, they operate farms and etc.

Before the abolition of slavery there was no real prison system in the United States. Punishment for crime consisted of physical torture, referred to as corporal or capital punishment. While the model prison in the United States was built in Auburn, New York in 1817, it wasn't until the end of the Civil War, with the official abolition of slavery, that the prison system took hold.

# YOU CAN BE A WINNER

The 13th Amendment officially abolished slavery for all people except those convicted of a crime and opened the door for mass criminalization. Prisons were built in the South as part of the backlash to Black Reconstruction and as a mechanism to re – enslave Black workers. In the late 19th century south, an extensive prison system was developed in the interest of maintaining the racial and economic relationship of slavery.

When slavery was legally abolished, a new set of laws called the Black Codes emerged to criminalized legal activity for African Americans. Through the enforcement of these laws, acts such as standing in one area of town or walking at night, for example, became the criminal acts of "loitering" or "breaking curfew." For which African Americans were imprisoned. As a result of Black Codes, the percentage of African Americans in prison grew exponentially, surpassing whites for the first time.

Just a few decades later, we are witnessing the return of all these systems of prison labor exploitation. Private corporations are able to lease factories in prisons, as well as lease prisoners out to their factories. Private corporations are running prisons – for profit. Government – run prison factories operate as multibillion dollar industries in every state, and throughout the federal prison system.

# REDEEM YOURSELF

Prison takes away power and control. It is a form of slavery that, unfortunately Black men are volunteering for in record numbers. The overseer is the judge, the slave masters are the correction officers. We have not ended racism in America, we have merely redesigned it.

In prison, the basis of the so called relationship between guards and prisoners, is that guards issue institutional orders and prisoners must comply – or the prisoners suffer the consequences. These consequences include prisoners being placed in solitary confinement or prisoners are forced to comply through violence inflicted on prisoners.

Similarity between the guards' role and the master's role can be found in the guards' absolute power to control the prisoner. This control is carried out by enforcing rules on the prisoner; closely watching the prisoner to ensure compliance with those rules; punishing, abusing and, if need be, eliminating the prisoner through banishment to solitary confinement or through violence.

"More African Americans are under correctional control today, then those who were enslaved in 1850." On the other hand, the resemblance of the prisoner to the slave is that both are subjected to strict rules, confined like animals, controlled, often brutalized physically as well as psychologically, and deprived of basic human rights.

YOU CAN BE A WINNER

A modern day slave system perpetrated, as a prison industrial complex or mass incarceration. How the system of mass incarceration works to trap African Americans in a cage can best be described viewing the system as a whole. The first stage is a vast amount of people swept into the criminal justice system by the police.

Modern – Day Slave Traits:

*A modern – day slave will neglect to educate himself, which in turn creates mental slavery. (During slavery, blacks were prohibited from learning to read or write. So, these days, everyone should take advantage of the opportunity to get an education).
*A modern – day slave will swindle and commit other crimes against their own people and others instead of helping to break the chains of poverty by earning an honest living.
*A modern – day slave will perpetuate self – hate through committing violence on people of his same ethnicity, such as black – on – black violence, including murder, which is a form of genocide.
*A modern day – slave will deal, buy and use drugs that will make him and others function as slaves (addicts) to drugs, slaves to misery and slaves to defeat.
*A modern – day slave will adopt the wicked ways of the slave master, who disrespected and abused women.

# REDEEM YOURSELF

*A modern – day slave will abandon his children – leaving them for someone else to raise just as the old masters abandon Black children by selling them off to other slave owners, not caring about their fate.
*A modern – day slave will foolishly commit crimes that cause him to end up behind bars, incarcerated, in mental and physical bondage.

Prison labor has its roots in slavery. After the 1862 – 1865 Civil War, a system of "hiring out prisoners" was introduced in order to continue the slavery tradition. Freed slaves were charged with not carrying out their sharecropping commitments (cultivating someone else's land in exchange for part of the harvest) or petty thievery – which were almost never proven – and were then "hired out" for cotton picking working in mines and building railroads.

Jim Crow racial division in the South 1865 – 1965 was a consequence, not a precondition of slavery, but once it was instituted it became detached from its initial function and acquired a social potency of its own.

Former Governor Davis Patterson, along with Senate Majority Leader Malcolm A. Smith and assembly Speaker Sheldon Silver announced an agreement calling for reform of the State's Rockefeller Drug law. Under the new laws, judges would now be able to impose sentences that fit the crime and the individual rather than a statue.

These new laws would allow judges the discretion to divert drug – addicted offenders into treatment – including the Shock incarceration program and Willard residential drug treatment. Prisons will be used to house the real offender and not those who really need help. The object seems to be to treat rather than punish, thus hopefully ending the cycle of addiction.

Emancipation thus created a double dilemma for Southern white society: how to secure anew the labor of former slaves, without whom the region's economy would collapse, and how to sustain the cardinal status distinction between whites and persons of color.

During the post – Civil War period, Jim Crow racial segregation laws were imposed on every state, with legal segregation in schools, housing, marriages and many other aspects of daily life. "Today, a new set of markedly racist laws is imposing slave labor and sweatshops on the criminal justice system, now known as the prison industry complex."

Human rights organizations, as well as social ones, are condemning what they are calling a new form of in humane exploitation in the United States, where they say a prison population of up to two million – mostly Black and Latino – are working for various industries for a pittance.

State's budget cuts have taken away educational opportunities in prisons.

# REDEEM YOURSELF

Teachers were laid off. College correspondence courses and vocational training have been cut drastically.

All these changes signify fewer opportunities for inmates to educate themselves and become more productive citizens when release back into society. If inmates are not given the opportunity to learn new skills in prison, how can you expect them to become law – abiding citizens upon release and reentry into society?

The prison system should reinstate education courses for inmates. The government ended education opportunities years ago. People coming out of prison with a G.E.D. or a college degree have a much greater chance of finding a job and staying out of prison.

If inmates had the opportunity to further their education and skills while in prison, fewer inmates would end up back in prison after release. Prisons then wouldn't be so over crowed. When inmates leave prison with a G.E.D., college degree, or vocational training skills, they have a better chance at making it in society.

What people may not realize is that cuts to prison education not only effect inmates but also society outside prison walls. When people who didn't further their education are released from prison, many people will return to their old life style of crime.

# YOU CAN BE A WINNER

If the public doesn't take note, of the fact that the success of inmates in prison will eventually help our society and communities in the long run. They should not expect the crime rate or the amount of money they pay in taxes for housing prisoners to go down.

Politicians must be asked, "Is this the best way they have to respond to this problem? To spend over sixty – two million dollars a year, to take men out of these communities and house them somewhere, knowing that they will all come back," not with skills and rehabilitation, but burdened with more barriers to life fulfillment than when they went in.

More attention is needed for aiding prisoners who seek to acclimate to life on the outside once their time has been served. Each year around six hundred fifty thousand people are released from prison, most with only enough money for a bus ticket. With little access to resources, a return to criminal behavior is more than likely.

Two thirds of the inmates released from U.S. prisons are rearrested within three years of their release and more than half end up back in prison. With a recidivism rate that exceeds 50 percent and the costs of incarceration – not to mention the costs to society for crime – you'd think that public officials would have come up with a better way to deal with this situation than the revolving door that it has become.

# REDEEM YOURSELF

If ye abide in me, and my words abide in you, ye shall ask what ye will, and it shall be done unto you
.

John 15:7

"Every person in America who is convicted of a misdemeanor or a felony receives a life sentence. Every person, "A person may or may not serve time. They may plea bargain and receive probation in lieu of incarceration program."

But whether they are in prison or not, it's the outcomes of that conviction where the problem lies. Because after you've served your time in prison, or after you've completed your parole or your probation that is what we call 'collateral consequences, or what they call "civil disabilities" or "conditional punishment" begin to take control."

A released prisoner is not a free man. Prior to the expiration of his maximum term, he is a ward of the Parole Board, subject to its control and care. Parole is not freedom. A parolee is a convicted criminal who has been sentence to a term of imprisonment, and who has been allowed to serve a portion of that term outside prison walls.

Parolees are assigned to a unique status in our legal system, neither physically imprisoned nor free to move at will.

# YOU CAN BE A WINNER

"A paroled prisoner can hardly be registered as a free man; he already lost his freedom by due process of law and, while paroled, he is still a convicted prisoner who's tentatively assumed progress towards rehabilitation."

They are different from other citizens and they may in certain circumstances, possess fewer constitutional rights. The difference in status and protection is based on the fact that parolees have been convicted of a crime and are still serving their sentence while on parole, albeit not within prison walls.

Once you are labeled a felon, you're trapped for the rest of your life and subject to many of those old forms of discriminations in job applications, rental agreements, loan applications, school applications, education grants and petitions for licenses. Those labeled felons can even be denied the right to vote and petition for licenses.

Those who have been incarcerated are forever marked as second class citizens, unable to participate fully in our so – called democratic society – unable to vote, to hold office, to get financial aid to go to college, to receive social service.

"Inmates will be discriminated against legally, for the rest of their lives, denied employment, housing, education, and public benefits.' Lack of education is the gate way to a lifetime of limited opportunity and a path way to prison and poverty.

# REDEEM YOURSELF

Most people released from prison return to their home communities. With criminal records haunting their every move, they face immense hurdles trying to find a job. Without employment, without a steady income, many return to criminal activities to survive and end up back in prison.

The national Urban League's 2009 State of Black America report notes that African Americans remain twice as likely as White Americans to be unemployed, three times more likely to live in poverty and more than six times as likely to be incarcerated.

The national unemployment rate for males without a high school education is 24 percent. People coming out of prison with a criminal record and no high school education are virtually unemployable. So why don't we have educational programs in prison? The key to employment for the formerly incarcerated is the acquisition of education skills.

We know that the unemployment problems for the black male are only extensions of equally deep concerns about mass incarceration and poor educational system. Actually, the system feeds off one another, for the black male attending the underfunded inner city school is far more likely to end up in the unemployment line. He also has a very good chance of ending up in prison.

# YOU CAN BE A WINNER

And yet there remains an expectation that prisoners can come back into society and become a productive law abiding – citizen. And yet they have every possible restriction directed to make that virtually impossible.

A 1996 law made a loss of eligibility for food stamps and other benefits a lifetime sentence for those convicted of a drug felony. The same change in federal law affected a federal housing regulation which that allows public housing facilities to evict any person or member of the families of any person convicted of a drug crime.

Other barriers to employment include an inability to use marketable skills. One can imagine that a barber in prison, cutting hair for a demanding clientele, would have the experience to work in a shop or possible start his own business. But he or she cannot do that in certain states and New York is one of them.

A large majority of prisoners are not the "violent predators' we are conditioned to believe. More than 70 percent of prisoners are locked up for non – violent crimes, most for drug offense or low – level property crimes.

While many prisoners only need drug or alcohol counseling or help finding jobs, the government instead chooses to incarcerate people. Rehabilitation programs cost far less and are more effective than prison.

# REDEEM YOURSELF

Imagine the challenges that many former prisoners are facing, as they try to stitch their lives together in these dire economic times. For many, the stresses must be enormous. It is important to address mental health and substance abuse issues.

The drug provision of the 1998 Higher Education Act delays or denies federal financial aid to anyone convicted of a state or federal drug offense. The Coalition for Higher Education Act Reform reports that "since taking effect in the fall of 2000, more than one hundred seventy five thousand students have been denied aid.

These young people, who have already been punished for their offenses, are now dropping out of school or reducing their course loads, because they cannot afford the high cost of tuition." It does not promote public safety to have young people uneducated and feeling helpless.

After receiving little treatment or guidance within prison, ex – cons are released to the street with only a few dollars in their pockets. These individuals have not only lost precious time to build a career, family, and friends, but they also face the stigma of being ex – cons. As a result, it is not surprising that more than 60 percent of people released from prison commit a crime after being released.

# YOU CAN BE A WINNER

No one is without a blemish and it is not something to be ashamed of. It's a reminder of a wounded past that can be used to heal others. We all have been damaged, but it should not be a reason to be discouraged. There is always a choice to be buried in depression or we can use the situation to become a better person and be a good example.

Inmates are excited about obtaining their freedom and returning to society and seeing love ones. You have made up your mind to be a law abiding citizen and to do the right thing. You have decided to be a parent to the children, look for a job and receive an education.

One of the biggest challenges is the fact that men want to fulfill their role as providers, but cannot find gainful employment. This is exacerbated by the fact that some of the young fathers are ex – offenders and our society is not forgiving, so even after they have served their time.

People will often become discouraged, due to these situations or circumstances. You are unable to find a job, or seek financial benefits, and you do not have money to support yourself. You are confronted with a dilemma that your family and spouse do not understand. Therefore you have exceeded their patience.

You now assume a negative behavior, and unbeknownst to you, you have begun to give up.

# REDEEM YOURSELF

No longer can you cope with being disrespected or denied an opportunity to better yourself. Society has a way of keeping people down, or denying individuals an opportunity to succeed in life, but you should not allow the system to win.

Often when you've been away from free society for a long period of time and lose contact with the outside world; it's easy to buy into the notion, that you no longer have a role or a place in society; it's even easier to believe that you have no role or place in your community.

The problem with this way of thinking is threefold: First, it causes you to give up on yourself and lose all hope. Second, it causes you to go through life without a sense of purpose or direction. And third, it causes you to spiral down the nothing – left – to – lose path. And we've already established what happens when you allow yourself to feel like you've got nothing left to lose.

There comes a time when you will have to choose between saving face and saving your freedom. For the average man, this is no easy task. But here is where you must decide whether you are going to be the average kind of man who loses his head at the slightest provocation, or the self – disciplined kind of person who thinks long and hard before he reacts.

# YOU CAN BE A WINNER

Why is this important strategy? Because as soon as you've made up your mind to stay on the straight and narrow path, life will send a situation your way, to see if you are serious about staying out of trouble, even when trouble finds you.

You ought to remain strong and determined. You should redefine your worth; so search deep within yourself; you decide what skill or talent needs to be developed. You may have a desire to speak, to share your experiences, in order to help people. Attend "Toastmasters' and train to become a public speaker.

Do you want to become an entrepreneur and conduct your own business? You have a business idea, so make your dream a reality and become the boss. There are various organizations that will help. You may decide to learn a building trade.

"Government grants provide ex – offenders with career skills, and help them establish small business." The U.S. Department of labor announced the availability of nearly twelve million dollars in grants that are earmarked for job training and life enrichment skills for ex – offenders.

Under a provision in President Barack Obama's Workforce Investment Act, dozens of grants will be awarded through a competitive process to various non – profit and faith – based community organizations.

# TRIBULATION

African people were stolen from their homes, locked in chains and taken across an ocean. And for more than two hundred years, their blood and sweat would help to build the richest and most powerful nation the world has ever known.

The conditions of capture and sale were crushing to Africans, and they were helpless in the face of superior force. The marched to the coast, sometimes for one thousand miles, with people shackled around the neck, under whip and gun, were death marches, in which two of every five Africans died.

They were packed aboard the slave ships, in spaces not much bigger than coffins, chained together in the dark, in the wet slime of the ship's bottom, choking in the stench of their own excrement.

# REDEEM YOURSELF

Some killed others in desperate attempts to breath. Slaves often jumped over board to drown rather than continue suffering.

Under these conditions, perhaps one of every three Africans transported overseas died, but the huge profits (often double the investments on one trip) made it worthwhile for the slave trader. On the coast, they were kept in cages until they were picked and sold.

African people were brought to America as slaves to pick cotton, tobacco and sugar cane. America's dilemma today is what to do with thirty six million Black American descendants of slaves, who were shipped to American shore four hundred years ago, for their economic value yet whose heirs today have lost that value? While America might have once considered shipping Black Americans back to Africa that is no longer a practical or palatable option.

By 1800, ten to fifteen million blacks had been transported as slaves to America, representing perhaps one – third of those originally seized in Africa. It is roughly estimated that Africa lost fifty million human beings to death and slavery in those centuries we call the beginnings of modern western civilization, at the hands of slave traders and plantation owners in Western Europe and America, the countries deemed the most advanced in the world.

Slaves lived in small wooden shacks.

# TRIBULATION

They had one set of clothes, which they wore until they could not mend them anymore. The slave owner fed them the least expensive food available – usually corn meal or grits. Meat was a special treat reserved for holidays.

Despite over all harsh conditions and the absence of freedom, slaves were not just powerless victims of their owners and the slave system. Slave families and communities became very important institutions. The slave's cabins (or 'quarter") provided one of the few places where slaves could do more or less free from constant supervision by slave overseers. There the slaves created a vibrant social and cultural life.

The life of a slave was a life of hard work. Most slaves worked from sun – up – to sun down, six days a week. Some slaves worked in the master's home cleaning, cooking, or taking care of the children. Most slaves worked in Southern cities, working at a variety of skilled trades as well as common laborers.

A slave's day usually consisted of long hours of physical labor. For a field hand, the work day usually began before dawn and ended after sun set. Slaves worked under constant supervision and the threat of physical punishment by their overseers. And through their lives were circumscribed in many significant ways, they sought to make the best of their circumstances.

Slaves were made to work by "overseers."

# REDEEM YOURSELF

There were men who managed the slaves and beat them if they did not work hard enough. Some slaves ran away and were able to reach the North, where they could be free. Most escaped slaves did not make it very far before being chased down.

The master knew that Negros imported from Africa had to be broken into bondage; that each succeeding generation had to be carefully trained. This was no easy task, for the slaves rarely submitted willingly.

The system was psychological and physical at the same time. The slaves were taught discipline, were impressed again and again with the idea of their own inferiority to "know their place," to see blackness as a sign of subordination, to be awed by the power of the master, to merge their interest with the master's, destroying their own individual needs.

Some slaves also fought back against the owners. They almost lost their lives. Slaves who did not run away or fight back found other ways to resist cooperating. They worked slowly, broke their tools, pretended not to understand instruction, or pretended to be sick.

Slaves were, by law, simply the property of their owners. When the owners wanted to sell slaves, they did. That meant that no slave could be sure when a father, mother, husband, wife, or child might be taken away – forever.

# TRIBULATION

Slaves who were sold to new owners had no way of telling their families where they had been taken to.

Willie Lynch "The Making of a Slave." The speech was delivered by Willie Lynch on the Bank of the James River in the colony of Virginia in 1712. Lynch was a British slave owner in the West Indies. He was invited to the colony of Virginia in 1712 to teach his methods to slave owners there. The term "lynching" is delivered from his name.

I caught the whiff of a dead Negro slave hanging from a tree, a couple miles back. You are not only losing valuable stock by hangings, you are having uprisings, and slaves are running away, your crops are sometimes left in the fields too long for maximum profit. You suffer occasional fires, your animals are killed.

Gentlemen, you know what your problems are; I do not need to elaborate. I am not here to enumerate your problems; I am here to introduce you to a method of solving them. In my bag here, I have a full proof method for controlling your Negro slaves. I guarantee every one of you, that if installed correctly, it will control the slaves for at least three hundred years.

My method is simple. Any member of your family or your overseer can use it. I have out lined a number of differences among the slaves; and I take these differences and make them bigger. I use fear, distrust and envy for control.

# REDEEM YOURSELF

I shall assure you that distrust is stronger than trust and even stronger than adulation, respect or admiration.

Slavery (1619 – 1865). Slavery is a highly malleable and versatile institution that can be harnessed to a variety of purposes, but in the Americas property – in – Person was geared primarily to the provision and control of labor. By the close of the 18$^{th}$ century, slavery had become self – reproducing and expanded to the fertile crescent of the Southern interior, running from South Carolina to Louisiana, where it supplied a highly profitable organization of labor for cotton production and the basis for a plantation.

Jim Crow (South, 1865 – 1965) racial division was a consequences, not a precondition, of us slavery, but once it was instituted it became detached from its initial function and acquired a social potency of its own.

Emancipation thus created a double dilemma for Southern white society; how to secure anew the labor of former slaves, without whom the region's economy would collapse, and how to sustain the cardinal status distinction between whites and persons of color.

By the 1800's, many white Americans viewed slavery as wrong. "Abolitionists" were people who worked to ban slavery; however, people in the South depended on slave workers. They knew that if they lost slave labor, they would lose most of their wealth.

174

# TRIBULATION

African American slavery was a thriving institution, especially in the South. One of the primary reasons for slavery was to make cotton production much more profitable and attractive to farmers in the South.

Harriet Tubman was a soldier, humanitarian, and Union spy during the American Civil War. She made thirteen missions to rescue slaves, using the network of anti slavery activists and safe houses from the South through the wild terrains of New York State known as the Underground Railroad.

The Underground Railroad changed the odds, helping more than thirty thousand slaves run away to the North, and to Canada. As a first step, volunteers with the Underground Railroad would sneak onto plantations in the South; they would find slaves who wanted to run away, often persuading those who were afraid.

They would lead small groups on foot or put them in wagons using secret paths and travel at night so they wouldn't be caught. In the day time, the slaves would stay at a safe house, where the owner had volunteered to help.

The next day the group would set out again, reaching a new home each night. Sometimes they would travel by boat or train, averaging about fifteen miles every day. Volunteers donated money for tickets and clothing for the run a ways. Ohio was the state with the most routes from South to North

# REDEEM YOURSELF

"I would have been able to free more slave, if they only knew they were slaves." How sad to be bound and not even know it. You can't even consider freedom if your mind is captive. Your thoughts determine your actions and you will only accomplish what you believe is possible.

One of the best – known workers on the Underground Railroad was Harriet Tubman. She escaped from slavery herself, but she wanted to help all slaves to be free. She went back to her old slave home and helped her family escape. She came back again and again, leading more than three hundred slaves to freedom.

When she became old, she said, "I was conductor of the Underground Railroad for eight years, and I can say what most conductors can't say – I never ran my train off the track and I never lost a passenger."

Slaves knew that there were laws against slavery in the Northern States. And they knew which way North was. But they also knew that running away was a crime. A slave who ran away once could expect to be beaten terribly – as a punishment, and as a way of reminding other slaves not to try it. A slave who tried to run away a second or third time could legally be put to death.

The South was also patrolled by police and professional slave catchers on horseback.

# TRIBULATION

A slave on foot who did not know where he was going or have anywhere to hide was usually caught within a day or two of running.

In the 1800's, more people began speaking out against slavery. Most – but not all – of the people who wanted it to be illegal were in the North. But the slave owners in the South did not agree. They depended on slave work to make money. Although many Northerners wanted the South to change, they did not want to force them to do so. The two sides tried to find a compromise, but none lasted. In the end, they fought a war – the Civil War – that settled the issue permanently.

During the war, President Abraham Lincoln decided the time had come to take the risk of telling the South what to do. In 1862, he wrote the "Emancipation Proclamation." "Emancipation" means freedom, and a "proclamation" is a statement made by a ruler, like a President.

From our American Revolution to the Civil War through the adoption of the Thirteenth Amendment, ending slavery, the Fourteenth Amendment, extending citizenship to all persons born or naturalized in the United States, applying the Bill of Rights to the states, apportioning representation to include the ex – slaves, and invalidating all debts for the emancipation of slaves, the Fifteenth Amendment, giving the right to the American Constitutional movement, freedom has been granted, seemingly.

# REDEEM YOURSELF

Lincoln said: "My paramount object in this struggle is to save the Union, and is not either to save or to destroy slavery. If I could save the Union without freeing any slave, I would do it; and if I could save it by freeing all the slaves, I would do it; and if I could do it by freeing some and leaving others alone, I would also do that."

His intentions of fighting the South did not lie with abolishing slavery, but to save the Union. Even though Lincoln died on April of 1865, the Thirteenth Amendment which abolished slavery was not instituted until eight months later, nearly three years from his "slave freeing" Emancipation Proclamation.

We hold these truths to be self evident: that all men are created equal; that they are endowed by their creator with certain inalienable rights; that among these are life, liberty, and the pursuit of happiness; that to secure theses rights, consent of the governed; that whenever any form of government becomes destructive of these ends, it is the right of the people to alter or to abolish it, and organizing its powers formulated in Washington, D.C. in the chamber of the House of Representatives.

African – Americans lost much more than freedom. We lost our heritage and our culture. All those years we worked for slave owners for free, whites were increasing their wealth and excelling in education, while African Americans were punished just for reading.

# TRIBULATION

And the shame of this nation's past has always been an issue; it would prefer not to talk about. Conse - quently, for years the disgrace of the American brand of slavery has been neatly tucked away, heading in the clouded recesses of a national conscience that shudders when asked to recall how the nation was built.

Imported from the North where it had been experimented within cities, this regime stipulated that Blacks travel in separate trains, street cars and waiting rooms, that they reside in the slum neighborhoods and be educated in separate schools (if at all); that they patronize separate service establishments, use their own bathrooms and water fountains. That they pray in separate churches, receive medical care in separate hospitals and exclusively from colored staff, and that Blacks be incarcerated in separate cells, also buried in separate cemeteries.

But when slavery ended, their welcome was over. African – Americans may have been given freedom, but they were betrayed, lied to and cast away. No 40 acres, no mule, nothing. America's wealthy elite had decided it was time for them to disappear and they were not particular about how it might be done.

Black people who think they are free and that the four hundred years of chattel and psychology slavery has not negatively impacted our lives are wrong. Blacks should conclude that they are trespassers, because Blacks were imported into this country as slaves

179

# REDEEM YOURSELF

Slavery is being practiced by the system under color of law. Slavery four hundred years ago, slavery today, it's the same thing, but with a new name. They are making millions and millions of dollars enslaving Blacks, poor Whites, and others – people who don't even know they're being included.

"We must see now that the evils of racism, economic exploitation and militarism are all tied together. You can't really get rid of one without getting rid of the others. The whole structure of American life must be changed. America is a hypocritical nation and (we) must put (our) own house in order." "There must be a better distribution of wealth and maybe America must move toward a democratic socialism."

I hear many people say that white men will never allow us to be equal and that one person can't make a change. My response is if Fredrick Douglas, Harriet Tubman, Nat Turner, Rosa Parks, Malcolm X and Dr. Martin Luther King Jr. would have said the same thing, we would still be on someone's plantation. To some it may be true that one person can't make a difference, but one person can start a movement to make a change.

Many young people believe that slavery never existed. Africans were kidnapped from their native land Africa, and brought to America in chains.

# TRIBULATION

African Americans have no knowledge of their culture, or what their ancestors endured for centuries, and the situations that came with slavery.

Freedom is a beautiful thing we take for granted, I hurt inside knowing our ancestors sacrificed enormous losses and abuse to achieve privileges that children take for granted. Wake up Black people, get together and stick together like other races.

The biggest challenge facing African Americans is to overcome the ruminants of Slavery. Despite our enslavement more than four hundred years ago, our ancestors never gave up. They had faith the cream would once again rise to the top. A sense of hopelessness seems to have invaded our spirits. We are headed back to the plantation. Millions of Black men are already behind bars.

Juneteenth represents June 19, the day in 1865, when enslaved Africans in Texas found out that there had been a law passed ending slavery in the United States in 1863. Many more Africans found out much later than that. But symbolically, Juneteenth is a holiday when Black people celebrate their freedom, liberation and achievement.

Whether it is New Year's Eve or "Watch Night" or "freedom Eve," the Black Community in America celebrates Freedom from slavery as of 11:59 p.m. December 31, 1862.

# REDEEM YOURSELF

"On that night, Blacks came together in churches and private homes all across the nation, awaiting news that the Emancipation Proclamation had actually become law."

Then, at the stroke of midnight, it was January 1, 1863, and according to Lincoln's promise, all slaves in the Confederate States were legally free. "When the actual news of freedom was received later that day, there were prayers, shouts and songs of joy as people fell to their knees and thanked God."

So, Black folks in America have gathered annually on New Year's Eve since the earliest days, praising God for bringing us safely through another year and praying for the future. Certainly, those traditional gatherings were made even more poignant by the events of 1863 which brought freedom to the slaves and the year of jubilee.

Many generations have passed since and most of us were never taught the African American History of Watch Night. Yet our traditions and our faith still bring us together, at the end of every year to celebrate once again "how we got over."

During National African American History Month, we recognize the extraordinary achievements of African Americans and their essential role in shaping the story of America. In honor of their courage and contributions, let us resolve to carry forward together the promise of America for our children.

# TRIBULATION

Now, therefore, I, Barack Obama, President of the United States of America, by virtue of the authority vested in me by the Constitution and the laws of the United States do hereby proclaim February 2, 2009 as National African American History Month. I call upon public officials, educators, librarians, and all people of the United States to observe this month with appropriate programs, ceremonies, and activities.

## REDEEM ONE'S SELF

Abraham Lincoln best described democracy as "government of the people, by the people, and for the people," For that government to be "by the people, however, it requires that the people decide who shall be their leaders.

Without free and fair elections, there can be no democratic society, and without that constant accountability of government officials to the electorate, there can, in fact, be no assurance of any other rights.

Blacks mostly voted Republican from after the civil War and through the early part of the 20$^{th}$ century.

# REDEEM YOURSELF

That is not surprising when one considers that Abraham Lincoln was the first Republican President, and the white, segregationist politicians who governed Southern States in those days were democrats. The Democratic Party did not welcome blacks then, and it was not until 1924 that blacks were even permitted to attend Democratic conventions in any official capacity.

By the time of the Civil War, most white men were allowed to vote, whether or not they owned property, thanks to the efforts of those who championed the cause of frontiersmen and white immigrants (who had to wait 14 years for citizenship and the right to vote, in some cases). Literacy tests, poll taxes, and even religious tests were used in various places, and most white women, people of color, and Native Americans still could not vote.

In 1866, the 14th Amendment to the Federal Constitution was passed, guaranteeing citizenship to the former slaves and changing them in the eyes of the law from 3/5 of a person to whole persons. Then, in 1869, the 15th Amendment guaranteed the right to vote to black men with most women of all races still unable to vote.

Under the Democratic Party, Blacks are powerless and have endorsed their own enslavement through voting. There has been a modification of the institution of slavery. Otherwise, the "badges of slavery" remain intact. Blacks are suffering from "badges of slavery."

# REDEEM ONE'S SELF

The landmark civil rights law, enacted in the wake of the brutal 1965 attack by local officials on civil rights advocate in Selma, Alabama, was designed to ease the way for Blacks to vote in the South, where white politicians made it hard for them to vote by imposing poll taxes, literacy tests and other obstacles. Its key provisions, including aid for Spanish – speaking voters were due to expire in August 2007.

There were no political options before 1965. Today, we enjoy voting rights if not political rights. Politics is about mind control, newspapers steer people in a certain direction and it is highly profitable to control minds. The most potent weapon in the hands of the oppressor is the minds of the oppressed. If you control the way a people think, you will also control the way a people act.

In 1965, President Lyndon B. Johnson signed the Voters Rights Act. This was created to allow Blacks the right to vote. In 1982, President Ronald Reagan signed an amendment to extend this right for an additional twenty – five years. Congress decided in 2007, whether or not Blacks should retain the right to vote.

The federal Voting Rights Act of 1965, enacted thanks to the pressures of Dr. Martin Luther King Jr. and a powerful civil rights movement, banned literacy tests and provided federal enforcement of voting registration and other rights in several Southern States and Alaska.

# REDEEM YOURSELF

"Dr. Martin Luther King Jr., had seen many years ago the obstacles that were deliberately placed before African Americans." Old and young men, women and children gave their lives to open the polls for all of those who could not vote. Black people and yes, Jewish people who stood alongside of those Black people faced dogs, hoses, angry white mobs and guns; they were willing to die for this right to express themselves at the polls and in the ways that human beings of dignity express themselves.

"As long as the mind is enslaved, the body can never be free. Psychological freedom – a firm sense of self – esteem – is the most powerful weapon against the long night of physical slavery," expressed Dr. Martin Luther King Jr. during his "Where Do We Go from Here," dissertation delivered at the Southern Christian Leadership Conference in Atlanta, GA., on August 16, 1967.

"The Black man will only be free when he reaches down to the inner depths of his own being and signs with the pen and ink of assertive manhood his own Emancipation Proclamation. And, with a spirit straining toward true self – esteem, (he) must boldly throw off the manacles of self – abnegation, and say to himself and to the world, "I am a man with dignity and honor, I have a rich and noble history."

The Voting Rights Act nearly expired and the Justice Department had failed to aggressively pursue allegations of disenfranchisement.

# REDEEM ONE'S SELF

By a vote of three hundred ninety in favor and 33 in opposition, the United States House of representatives passed the Voting Rights Reauthorization Bill, which includes key provisions that were set to expire in 2007.

"The right to vote is one of our nation's most sacred rights. We must not forget those who came before us, who made great sacrifices to ensure this right for everyone, regardless of race, income or literacy level."

Millions of Americans cannot vote because they were convicted of a felony sometime in their past. Nearly four million people are out of prison, having completed their sentences or been placed on parole or probation. They live in communities, work, pay taxes and raise families. Yet they remain disenfranchised.

In case you have not noticed, in many states there is a Republican majority in control, efforts are under way to restrict voting, whether by further limiting ex – felons from voting. The objective is to reduce the potential anti – Republican electorate. This is being done by demagogically and inaccurately crowing about alleged voter fraud.

Denying black and poor people their right to vote dramatically all decreased the political power of urban and minority communities. And "disenfranchising the head of a household can discourage his or her entire family from civic participation.

# REDEEM YOURSELF

In the 2008 election, we saw a level of voter participation unparalleled in our nation's history, with young people and communities of color. For the first time, Black women had the highest voter turnout rate among all racial, ethnic and gender groups, while the turn out rate of young Black voters was higher that of young voters, of any other racial or ethnic group.

Engaged voters in 2008 showed that our nation believes in hope and the possibilities of the American Dream. For too many, that dream remains unfulfilled. While schools crumble, the prison population soars, and hospitals close, we edge closer to being the first generation to be worse off than our parents.

President Barack Obama has inherited the fall of America as a great nation. The education institutions are falling apart, politics in a shamble, economics in a shamble. This man became president at a time like this, because much of the nation has failed its people and he's expected to deliver America from its disaster.

The Republicans are telling the entire nation, that they want to see the Obama's administrations fail. In other words they want to see American economy and people suffer, some even die as a result of the effects of recession or worst depression. I believe the Republican Party is the sort of American racism, bigotry and capitalistic exploitation, or human insensitivity. It's an organization for the wealthy and powerful.

# REDEEM ONE'S SELF

Voting was not an option for people of Color, or neither a gift people obtained. You would believe after all these hardships, that the voting rights would be law, and should not have to be renewed.

In short, Blacks are political wards of the Democratic Party. The Democratic Party selected the candidates and Blacks help elect them. This was our role on the plantation. Whites selected the crop and we picked it. Our voting rights are actually voting privileges. If voting were a right, it would be a constitutional fixture. Instead, it is a short – term lease. It must be renewed.

"I often wonder if President Barack Obama would've been elected, if the Voting Rights Act had not been renewed." This had to become a law in order for our right to vote to no longer be up for discussion, review or evaluation.

For me and many others, this was the first time we heard of this – this should concern people. What many Blacks before us fought and even died for, as well as the milestones that we, as Blacks have achieved, this can be taken away from us.

"Take obstacles and turn into opportunity."

# RESOURCES

These facilities are for men, women and youth from all walks of life. You might decide to utilize these resources, such as health, housing, rehab, education and employment.

(A)

Access Youth, Inc.
3259 Prospect Street, NW
Washington, DC 20007
Tel. 202-652-0287
www.accessyouthinc.org
Recognize the unlimited potential of each child and provides youth with resources, support, and services that empower them to transform themselves and make life choices that positively impact their future.

Alliance of Concerned Men
1424 16th Street, Suite 103
Washington, DC 20036
Tel. 202-462-9700
www.allianceofconcernedmenn.com
Provides social services, recreational activities for youth, and families' incarcerated or substance abuse.

Anchor House, Inc.
104-47 Bergen Street
Brooklyn, New York 11216
Tel. 718-771-0760
www.anchorhousenyc.org
Intensive long term (12-18 months) faith based residential treatment program for men and women.

(C)

California Coalition for Women Prisoners
1540 Market Street, Suite 490
San Francisco, CA 94102
Tel. 415-255-7036
www.womenprisoners.org
Raising public consciousness about the conditions
under which women in prison live and advocates for
positive changes. Promotes women's leadership and
gives voice to women prisoners, former prisoners, and
their families.

Centerforce
2955 Kerner Boulevard, 2nd Floor
Sam Rafael, CA 94901
Tel. 415-456-9980
www.centerforce.org
Services people incarcerated and their families. That
includes literacy, family support, education, parenting,
health and wellness.

COMAlert
210 Joralemon Street, 3rd Floor
Brooklyn, New York 11201
Tel. 718-250-5557
www.brooklynda.org
Offer through the Brooklyn District Attorney's office.
COMAlert provides drug treatment counseling, G.E.D.
completion and transitional housing and employment.

(D)

Delancey Street Foundation
100 Turk Hill Road
Brewster, NY 10509
www.delanceystreetfoundation.org
A residential self – help organization for drug addicts,
convicts and others in need. After an average of four
years – and a minimum stay of two years, residents
gain an academic education and three marketable
skills.

(E)

Exponents
151 West 26 Street, 3$^{rd}$ Floor
New York, NY 10001
Tel. 212-243-3434
www.exponents.org
Provides drug abuse treatment, HIV counseling, life
skills training, case management, outreach and risk
reduction services, and hosts an annual ex – offenders'
conference that teaches life skills and job readiness.

(F)

Families in Crisis, Inc.
30 Arbor Street, North Wing
Hartford, CT 06106
Tel. 860-231-2593
www.familiesincrisis.org
Through 4 offices statewide, provides services to
promote families' role in helping people in prison.

Rebuilds families, reduces crime, and prepares prisoners to be productive citizens through counseling and support, fatherhood and youth services, transportation.

Family Reentry, Inc.
9 Mott Avenue, Suite 104
Norwalk, CT 06850
Tel. 203-838-0495
www.familyreentry.org
Provides counseling, educational programs, and substance abuse. Youthful offender mentoring program matches males and females who are in prison with volunteer adults from the community.

Fortune Society
53 W. 23rd Street, 8th Floor
New York, NY 10010
Tel. 212-691-7554
http://fortunesociety.org
HIV education, counseling and case management, individual and group counseling, job training and placement, court advocacy, substance abuse treat – ment services, family counseling and parenting workshops, transitional housing, and aftercare services.

(G)

Good Help Program
Brooklyn Chamber of Commerce
25 Elm Place, Suite 200
Brooklyn, NY 11201
Tel. 718-871000
www.ibrooklyn.com/site/chamberdirect/goodhelp

This is a business – driven employment service designed to help businesses and unemployed residents. The organization works with employers to find job openings, screen potential employees, check references, and follow up with placements.

Green Hope Services for Women, Inc.
448 East 119<sup>th</sup> Street
New York, NY 10035
Tel. 212-996-8633
www.greenhope.org
Residential and day treatment for substance abuse and reentry services for women paroles.

(H)

House of Hope
P.O. Box 12113
Gainesville, FL 32604
www.hohinfo.org
A faith – based organization, offers shelter and job placement to recently released people with criminal records, substance abuse, anger management and spiritual counseling are also available.

(L)

Legal Action Center
225 Varick Street
New York, NY 10014
Tel. 212-243-1313
www.lac.org
Provides legal assistance to ex- offenders, addicts and alcoholics who feel discriminated against in employment.

(M)

Medgar Evers College CUNY Catch
1150 Carroll Street, Room 111
Brooklyn, NY 11225
Tel. 718-270-6407
http://ace.laguardia.edu/catch
Helps people ages 16 to 22 to transition back into the
community. Once enrolled in college, the program
offers career development and job search services as
well as substance abuse treatment referral.

Mentor/National Mentoring Partnership
1600 Duke Street, Suite 300
Alexandria, VA 22314
Tel. 703-224-2200
www.mentoring.org
Advocates for the expansion of mentoring and serve as
a resource for mentors and mentoring initiatives
nationwide.

(N)

National Fatherhood Initiative
101 Lake Forest Boulevard, Suite 360
Gaithersburg, MD 20877
Tel. 301-948-0599
www.fatherhood.org
Improve the well – being of children by increasing the
proportion of children growing up with involved
responsible and committed fathers. We strive to ensure
a brighter futher for America's youth. By equipping and
educating fathers, we're working on an issue that is at
the core of our nation's well – being.

(O)

Osborne Association
36 – 31 38<sup>th</sup> Street
Long Island City, NY 11101
www.osborneny.org
Serves people at all stages of the criminal justice
system and their children and families at community
sites. Services include substance abuse treatment,
employment placement and training programs, HIV and
risk reduction services, transitional planning and reentry
initiatives and family services.

(P)

Passage Home
712 W. Johnson Street
Raleigh, NC 27603
Tel. 919-843-0666
www.passagehome.org
This is a faith based, non – profit, community providing
housing and support services to low – income and
homeless families, including individuals with criminal
histories.

Project Return
2703 General De Gaulle Drive
New Orleans, LA 70114
Tel. 504-998-1000
www.projectretun.com
Services will be provided for substance abuse,
education, communication classes, life skills, job
training, and placement assistance. Public education

Network's School and Community Service Initiative
601 Thirteenth Street, NW
Washington, DC 20005
Tel. 202-628-7460
www.publiceducation.org
Addresses the challenge of meeting the non –
academic needs of children or help ensure that
students are at their best, academically and socially.
The initiative takes a child – centered, coordinated –
services perspective that recognizes the role of
schools, families, and community agencies in the lives
of children.

(R)

Ridge House, Inc.
275 Hill Street, Suite 281
Reno, NV 89501
Tel. 775-322-8941
Program provides a three – month residential
substance abuse treatment and an out patient program.

(S)

Second Chance/Strive
505 16th Street
San Diego, CA 92101
Tel. 619-239-1003
Serve individuals with a criminal history, long – term
unemployment, and homeless people.

(T)

The Doe Fund, Inc.
232 East 84<sup>th</sup> Street
New York, NY 10028
Tel. 212-628-5207
www.doe.org
Residents learn job skills training program. Ex –
offenders with immediate employment, substance
abuse counseling, housing and other services to assist
participants in overcoming joblessness and
homelessness.

Time for Freedom, Inc.
P.O. Box 819
Ocala, FL 34470
Tel. 352-351-1280
www.thefreedomhouse.org
Transitional housing and support for recently releases
men with criminal histories.

(W)

Women's Self Employment Project
11 S. LaSalle, Suite 1850
Chicago, Il 60606
Tel. 312-606-8255
www.wsep.net
Program provides entrepreneurial training to women
primarily from low – income and minority communities.
The organization is developing a pilot program for
clients with criminal records.

Women's prison Association
175 Remsen Street
Brooklyn, NY 11201
Tel. 718-637-6800
www.wpaonline.org
Assists women in adopting life skills needed to end involvement in the criminal justice system and to make positive, healthy choices for themselves and their families. Develop women's independent living skills and intensive case management for substance abuse.

Women in Need, Inc.
115 West 31$^{st}$ Street
New York, NY 10001
Tel. 212-695-4758
www.womeninneed.org
Provide ex – offenders and their families – who are homeless and disadvantaged. Offers the tools and guidance that allow families to return to their communities and live independently.


Women's Reentry Network
1468 W. 25$^{th}$ Street
Cleveland, OH 44113
Tel. 216-696-7535
Services include assessment, intensive case management, individual and group management, parenting classes, legal education, job readiness workshops and job placement service.

**Websites:**

www.knowmydepression.com
www.nimh.nih.gov

www.stresscenter.com
www.fathering.org
www.fathers.org
www.hivtest.org
www.thebody.com
www.orgformen.org
www.menshealthnetwork.org
www.bigbrothersbigsisters.org
www.menmentoringmen.com
www.aa.org
www.na.org
www.drugnet.net
www.dol.gov
www.nationalparenthelpline.org
www.yearup.org

Send order form with check or money order to:
Jerome Livingston
P.O. Box 170283
Brooklyn, NY 11217
Tel. 917-509-8274

Shipping Address:

Name: _____

Address: _____

City: _____

State: _____

Zip: _____

Telephone _____

Email: _____

| Product | Price | Quantity | Price |
|---|---|---|---|
| Redeem Yourself | $18.45 | _____ | _____ |
| Lust of a Dope Fiend | $13.50 | _____ | _____ |

(Shipping is included in prices) Total: _____

Please visit our web site
www.TheStrongWillSurvive.com

|

www.ingramcontent.com/pod-product-compliance
Lightning Source LLC
LaVergne TN
LVHW051510080426
835509LV00017B/2012